CONSTRUCTIVE
ETHICS

CONSTRUCTIVE
ETHICS

T. V. Smith

William Debbins

PRENTICE-HALL, INC.   A Spectrum Book

T. V. Smith (Ph.D., University of Chicago) is an author of international
reputation, having been editor for two decades of the *International Journal of Ethics*. Among his works are *Discipline for Democracy, Ethics of
Compromise, Live Without Fear,* and a series entitled *Philosophers Speak
for Themselves*. At present he is Maxwell Professor Emeritus at Syracuse
University.

William Debbins (Ph.D., Syracuse University) compiled the bibliography
of T. V. Smith's writings in *Retrospect and Prospect,* edited by T. Denise
and M. Williams. Mr. Debbins is currently Assistant Professor of Philosophy at Elmira College.

PRINTED IN THE UNITED STATES OF AMERICA

16924-C

PREFACE

Ethics has to do with the study of Right and Wrong, of Good and Bad. Wherever men concern themselves with understanding their own duties or privileges, with appreciating the obligations or rights of others, there ethics is.

Our first duties were laid upon us from beyond. Our first goods, however, were discovered in us, by ourselves. We got into the habit of crediting each to the source whence it first derived, thus widening the breach between duties and values, between actions done because we ought and opportunities embraced because we wished. Since none of us has been privileged to grow up in a perfect society, nor to have had either paragons for parents or gods as teachers, each of these elements of morality has more or less fed upon itself, the two growing apart as they fed differently: rightness and duty coming from the expectations and demands of others; goods and values arising first from our mothers' milk and bubbling subsequently from other of our "erogenous" zones. Frequently these equally indigenous elements of morality have grown so apart as to bequeath each of us, if not a multitude of selves with much in-fighting, then at least an objective society with such division of moral labor as to perpetuate a widening gulf between its instrumentalities of power and its gentler agencies of perfection.

This great division sets our ethical task, as every psychiatrist knows and as every man of the world observes. It sets it both historically and psychologically. It is what life is mostly about, morally speaking: the welding together of our two great value-systems, at the high reward to us as individuals of measurably unified selves. If we cannot gain pure happiness, we may yet stay out of the insane asylum. That life is successful which can achieve at the end, what in this book we shall mean auspiciously now to further, that is, the harmony whose absence we lamented during adolescence as a simple but very sad lack. We would speed up if we can, but anyhow consummate before life is done, the vision of self-unity described by Confucius: "At fifteen my mind was bent on learning. At thirty I stood firm. At forty I was free from delusions. At fifty I understood the law of Providence. At sixty my ears were attentive to truth. At seventy I could follow my heart's desire without transgressing the law."

Such full self-possession it is the part of ethics to disclose to appreciation and help to provide through understanding. We are deeply minded in this book to do our part to bring into unison, with the Chinese sage, the heart's desire and the law of duty. What the task is in all its concreteness we may discern from a letter I am permitted to quote by a lady who wrote it to her mother when she was eleven. Save for its poignancy we could all probably match it out of our own experience.

I heard a sermon about letting go and depending on God this morning at church. Tonight we played bridge. I played with Grandmother. We were losing but I wanted Grandmother to be dummy. I depended on God that we should win because the preacher said that if you depended on God he would do it. We lost. Grandmother wasn't dummy so now what should I do? Believe in God and what the preacher said or say you can't depend on God? . . . I was so disappointed. Please write quickly.

At the other end of life Lady Astor at a recent birthday said that as a young person she used to worry that when she was old she would not be able to do what she wanted to do, but now that she was old, she no longer wanted to do it.

Attrition as well as creation has its uses.

CONTENTS

I.   THE MORAL AS THE RIGHT   1

1. THE RIGHT AS THE MANNERLY   3
2. THE RIGHT AS THE LEGAL   18
3. THE RIGHT AS THE NATURAL   28
4. THE RIGHT AS THE CONSCIENTIOUS   39
5. THE RIGHT AS THE RIGHT   49

II.   THE ETHICAL AS THE GOOD   59

6. THE GOOD AS THE PLEASURABLE   61
7. THE GOOD AS SELF-REALIZATION   73
8. THE GOOD AS THE ADVENTUROUS   82
9. THE GOOD AS THE GOOD   93

III.   THE MORAL LIFE AS SYNTHESIS   103

10. THE MEETING OF EXTREMES: THE RIGHT AND THE GOOD   105

POSTLUDE   THE WAY TO GET IS TO FORGET   117

BOOK I

THE MORAL AS THE RIGHT

One of the key-words of Ethics is the "Right." We say that an act is either right or wrong. We praise children for doing right. We punish adults for doing wrong. And we express our upward yearning as aspiration for rightness.

What precisely all this means is better concluded at the end than risked at the beginning. Definitions nurture the illusion of omniscience in simple minds, and in devotees of the logical they sometimes facilitate the all too easy presumption of grasping the substance when we have only been introduced to its symbol. All this we would avoid, avoid without shirking the responsibility of clarification. We can safely guess to begin with, that Right means something different from, and indeed a good deal more than, any term we may use in connection with it. Indeed if right meant simply and precisely something else, we should talk of that something else instead. Right, then, is right, whatever else we may say about it. It will pay us to remember this, without using the ease of the oracular to excuse us from further intellectual exertion.

Right is right, but, even so, it is such an important matter that we want to supplement our intuition of that fact with whatever else will fill out its profile. We want to know not only, or merely, the meaning of the concept; we want to be able to identify its essence in the ebb and flow of life, our own and others. We want to know what actions are right for us to do, what actions we may justly forbid others as wrong. We need, in short, all the guidance we can get upon duty, positive and negative.

Now it happens that words like these, "right" and "duty," describe our conduct from the point of view of others, and to that extent from the outside (it is at times quite an extent). Duty is not something which a man personally invents. "Rightness" is a quality if not socially derived, then

*at least socially informed. When we think of conduct purely from the
way it affects us individually, we more naturally speak of "good" and
"bad." But from the beginning we are members of families, then of play-
groups, school-groups, gossip-groups, church-groups, and at last of state-
groups. We get told what to do, and come to accept the telling as binding. To some extent we come to like, at least to tolerate, being told. Our
duty in fact arises largely from the expectations others have of us; what
"they" uniformly and confidently expect of us becomes, in general,
"right" for us to do.*

*Without trying to make the distinction between the "Right" and the
"Good" sharper than life makes it for each one, we must take account of
certain differences in point of view. This is the largest difference, and so
becomes the major distinction in ethics: the difference between the social
point of view (the Right) and the individual point of view (the Good).
Both views are natural, given the inevitable point of view; and both are
equally fruitful.*

*Using Rightness, then, as our initial approach to ethics, we discover
without delay that characteristically we try to expedite duty, as well as
clarify right, by identifying the Right, at different times and for different
purposes, with other notions. As we have said, it is not likely that any of
these other notions will exhaust our key-word, or fairly define it. But
jointly and severally they help to locate it, to fixate its spread; and therefore they become useful guides or clues to us in understanding the moral
life—and, specifically, in helping us to know and to do our duty.*

*In succession we shall consider now, in the order that seems easiest,
certain conceptions that have been in the West and are today associated
with the reality of our present concern, Morality as Rightness. This order
permits us at once to isolate two stages, to serve as introductory guide-
posts to our study of the Right. The first we shall unaffectedly call manners, the second law, letting any special meanings emerge as we proceed.
Beyond these we shall utilize other categories to come to quarters with
the Right, but these two concepts belong together and naturally come
first.*

THE RIGHT AS THE MANNERLY

Good manners clearly have much to do with morals, though just how much—and indeed just *how*—has long been debated. We wish to turn to positive account in the good life whatever manners have to offer.

That offering is, it would appear, at three levels. It is, first, an inner concern. Then as courtliness passes to its social vocation, it sojourns as long as it can at the level of like-mindedness: love and friendship, religion and art. Beyond that there lies the land of unlike-mindedness which, unless it be informed of etiquette, gets ruffled over with pure aggressiveness and bodies itself forth as war, in which men not only get killed but leave their culture criss-crossed for generations. So deep the dominance of conflict in life seemed, for instance, even to the wise and learned Justice Holmes, that the highest hope for mankind he was able to bequeath us was merely of a regime of "force mitigated so far as may be by good manners."

Good manners can certainly "mitigate" much, the current unlike-minded association, for example, between the Russians and the Democratic world. But before we exploit the fecundity of gentility for that harsher world of politics and diplomacy, for commerce and war, we shall in this chapter canvass the closer and lovelier plains of like-mindedness marked by education, friendship and love.

As a precondition for even this, however, let us remark specifically upon the self, and its hygiene. There is such a thing as good manners to oneself, when "the soul selects her own society, then shuts the door." Plato speaks of thinking as being "the soul's conversation with herself." Whoever is graciously at home to himself is best armored for the outer world. It is the man at outs with himself who is most likely to be rude to others. Good manners are, in an intimate sense, the hygiene of sanity. Self-respect does not arise from self-abuse but from self-help; and self-

3

respect is the precondition of right conduct to others, whether they be friends or enemies. That let us remember as we now proceed with caution toward the outer.

Under the Baconian title of "Manners Maketh Man," Mr. Harrison Smith, Publisher, wrote in an editorial for the *Saturday Review of Literature* (XXX:18, 1947) that "politeness as a lubricant and an anti-irritant has gone overboard today, and shrillness and violence reign." The article expressed a hope for new "codes of manners, founded on the dignity inherent in human nature"; and his appeal was to litterateurs for imaginative standards of gentility. "When chastity went out of the novelist's window and the baby, to use Mr. Cain's title, was thrown out of the icebox, the high-school girl or boy avidly reading to discover what life and love were like, found no substitute for their parents' outworn and outmoded conceptions of how the young should behave. . . . Love in our novels was no longer made with tender words couched in charming sentences; girls were grabbed, not tenderly embraced, and were seduced without the benediction of an introduction."

Whether Harrison Smith's editorial be overdrawn or not, it reminds us that good manners are not only an easy way to approach but also a fruitful way to introduce the ethics of duty. They are a means which, like all noble means, coalesce with the nobility of right ends. "When manners left the novel," says Smith, "so did polite or even intelligent conversation." If there were some magic way of restoring, or instating, good manners, we should thereby no doubt do much for morals. "Good manners" are a *form* of manners; and *manners* are custom become conscious and cultivated for their own sake. Not only so, but they represent custom made plural and, as it were, sparkling.

"The bedside manner" of doctors is but an easy symbol for the larger fact that the medical profession, any profession, has its own particular folk-ways, and these go to make up not a little of the given profession's ethics. It is not good manners—to continue for a moment with the medical illustration—for one doctor to call upon the patient of another doctor, unless a consultation has been properly arranged between the doctors. Protocol is required to heal a professional breach, or bad blood attends the carelessness. Homeopathically speaking, custom, and only custom, can cure the ills of custom.

There is an ordinary dividing line between manners and morals—morals being manners that are important, and manners being procedures that involve "taste," whose breach stops short of any suspicion of turpitude. Where the one ends and the other begins, however, nobody knows in the concrete. "Importance" is a matter of time and place, and sometimes

"taste" is itself all-important. There is something to be said for the auda-
cious claim of Emily Post, that "etiquette must . . . include ethics." However that be, the two together represent a continuity of development all
the way from kindness to heroism, and, on the negative side, all the way
from boorishness to brutishness. Nor is their relation, positive or negative,
merely linear; it is more mixed than that. What is admittedly "bad" can,
for instance, be done *in such a manner* as to mitigate its evil, and what is
"good" can be so crabbedly performed as to rob it of anything save the
merest mantle of virtue. Lord Chesterfield thought, indeed, that men in
general are, as he says, "easier won by unprofitable courtesies than by
churlish benefits."

It was Robin Hood's gallantry—one sees it in America's Southwest in
the story of the James Brothers—that has made for fame, perhaps as much
as the "moral" fact that Robin Hood robbed the rich to succor the poor.
An automobile thief lately left on your author's mind a favorable impression, in spite of your author's aversion to thievery, because instead of
wrenching the radio out of the car, this thief carefully unscrewed the
radio, leaving the dashboard unscratched, and placed the screws neatly
on the floor of the car—all ready for the installation of a new radio.

Without suggesting that manners are all there is of morals, it is necessary now to make plain that rightness is to some degree determined by
the mannerly. The student will almost certainly be surprised, once his
attention has been called to it, to observe for himself how large this degree
is. As the *Encyclopaedia of Social Sciences* soberly and sagely remarks,
"Etiquette always involves respect for the persons to whom it is addressed.
A breach of it is therefore a slight. This consequence may be avoided if
the person who commits it excuses himself." So much of ordinary ethics
is simply good manners, especially in the student's world, that he who is
genteel has a headstart on mastering what more remains of ethics. Since
good manners include the portion of ethics that is in itself most attractive,
emphasis upon etiquette is a natural and effective introduction to what is
more arduously right. Parents are even wiser than teachers in studying
and insinuating the ethical from this more gracious point of view.

AN ILLUSTRATION FROM PEDAGOGY

A businessman called recently, first by telephone and then at my office,
some twenty-five years after having had with me an undergraduate course
in ethics. As we talked, our past relations came back to me vaguely but
pleasantly enough at the fringes to lead me to ask him, quite innocently,
what had drawn us together, man-to-man, in the first place. He expressed

surprise that I had forgotten the tensional beginning of our friendship. He had, he said, failed every test in my course but came up on the final examination with an all but perfect score. I had called him in, talked about things in general, but at last had asked him many specific questions about ethics. He finally guessed my motive and explained that he had been completely at sea during most of the course. He had failed the specific tests not for want of information but for lack of perspective. He had not understood the textbook at all and could not understand the instructor nor what ethics in general was about. At length, angry at textbook, instructor and self alike, he had sat down, read carefully, thought hard, and had at last got for himself the clue. The clue in hand, all else as usual came easy; and, fugitive facts falling now into place, he had found the final examination a welcome chance to pull it all together.

Seeing clearly, from the oral interview, that he knew what was what, I welcomed his explanation with such glad release from the odious duty of charging him with cheating that I became friendly for the relief he brought me and he became friendly for the courtesy of my abstention from the easy way of suspicion. Truth to tell, I had grown used to such floundering on the part of students and had learned from sad experience the normal inutility of charging students with cheating or with anything else which is bad. A teacher who fails has, if not only himself, then at least himself, much to blame for any abortive outcome of a relationship so high in promise of mutual growth and deepening affection.

ETIQUETTE BETWEEN THE TEACHER
AND HIS COMMUNITY

Conditioning the flowering of student-teacher relations is in many senses the relation the teacher sustains toward his larger community. There will be little politeness toward the teacher at school if the students hear outside that the teacher is either a hypocrite or a mouse. And the student does sometimes pick up one or the other impression about the teacher from homes, streets, playground, or adult conversations in general. At a time when the tides are turning in America against "liberalism," the students, quick in imagination and ready in sympathy, are all too prepared to suspect that in discussions of moot issues the teacher is not sharing with them his true opinions. That suspicion is fatal to a frank interchange, for students not only thus lose interest in discussion but lose respect for the teacher also.

In protection of their calling, as well as in defence of themselves, teachers should be courageous men and women who can match their convictions with candid affirmation or adroit change of venue. Chronic timorousness was the worst damage we found that totalitarianism had done to the teaching profession in Italy, Germany, and Japan.

Nothing quite like that exists in America, but the domestic situation is far from conducive to courageous teaching in many communities. Anything short of sectarian orthodoxy is in some sections frowned upon; and in other sections economic radicalism is the sticking point (which may mean anything from I-fear-him-a-communist- to I-am-certain-that-I-don't-like-him). The teacher owes good manners to his community, but he does not owe subserviency to it. He owes deference to his job but not at the price of self-respect. He should not be hypocritical but he may take joy in being resourceful; and the community will be doubly repaid if it allows the teacher to do his own adjusting rather than getting the kind of accommodating, or lack of it, that self-appointed guardians of any kind of orthodoxy think ought to be required of public servants.

As to religious orthodoxy, which the Constitution forbids to be made a test of public employment, the teacher is privileged through courtesy to save as much as possible the religious impulse from degrading itself in sectarianism. Much may be done here through kindness strategically employed. Jefferson, it will be remembered, refused categorically to disclose his religious beliefs, not because they were not worthy but because he would not, by answering unconstitutional impudence, encourage the asking of questions which good manners in a democracy forbid.

Here indeed is the teacher's opportunity, whatever form the orthodoxy take, to demonstrate to the community the social manners of courage and the etiquette of responsibility in tensional times: by knowing what to keep to himself, what to share, and how to do the one in self-respect and the other with magnanimity. It is a difficult duality: what to do with the surplusage of ideals over the possibility which the community offers to action prompted in the name of this surplusage. Clearly, one is not, in good democratic manners, privileged to say all that he thinks. The liberal errs who perpetrates such candor. The fact that he believes something very honestly and very deeply lays no certain duty upon him to shout his convictions to a community that prefers its own. As he would not himself be pressed, let him not seek to proselyte. Proselyting is beyond the pale of good manners, on whatever side it arises. Good manners run to their richest flowering indeed in knowing what to keep to oneself. Not to share everything but to share honestly and candidly what one does share, that is here the golden mean.

What is here said of the teacher is equally true of other professionals who serve the community. A doctor or a minister who thinks that he may tell what he knows can easily become a community menace. Nor is it different with the lawyer. Only the teacher is not supposed to have a private life, in which social distance from the community can be maintained. The other professions have indeed well recognized "privileged communications," whose secrecy the law itself will protect. As the teacher becomes more of a professional, he will learn better how to be a good servant of the actual community without ceasing to be a prophet of the better community.

WIDER REFLECTIONS UPON MORALS AS MANNERS

Manners are many. This grows more manifest every day, not only inside a given community with its pluralism of professions and non-professional groups but also between the larger communities themselves. In a pinch, it is now only a week-end around the world. The maxim "When in Rome do as Romans do" means also "When in Paris do as Parisians do." It arose at a time, however, when Paris and Rome were far apart, and Washington was yet undreamed of. That was a time when a man stayed at whatever place he arrived, at least long enough to recover from the fatigue of his journey. This gave him occasion to learn something of the manners of his new place and to profit from accommodating himself to its own idiom.

We now race on without settling down, and the whole world is the moving locale of our multitudinous manners. This mobility lends added necessity, if that be possible, to the question of manners, which are the visible manifoldness of custom. "Life's jostle and jar," as one book on etiquette phrases it, is not necessarily lessened through cosmic extension. The new mobility, to which one cannot merely surrender without inviting dissipation in which integrity would evaporate, lays two obligations upon us, if we are to turn it to fullest moral account. One of the obligations lies in that domain of the moral which is usually thought of as ethics proper, but which we here prefer to regard as merely what ethics is in addition to all else that it is. It is the necessity of having at the core of our many-fringed characteristics, a solid, even a stubborn self. Men are pusillanimous unless they can remain themselves while becoming other things to other men. But this can await its treatment under conscience, a proper place to consider integration of character.

The other obligation falls logically here in our discussion of manners. It is that we must develop a cosmopolitan spirit as quickly as possible and, meantime, must improve our tolerance of the various sartorial makeshifts of the human spirit. There are those who believe that a common gentility, cosmic in classlessness, must arise—such as the "cult of the comrade," as during the French Revolution there arose the "cult of the citizen"—to match the new mobility and to avert the new menace of atomic fission.

Such rendition is possible. Before surrendering, however, to cultural sameness, on a universal scale, one may remember that there have been those who thought, perhaps are still those who think, that uniformity of that dominant custom of mankind, language, is imperative before any international good can come. Possibly, but not probably. It was once good manners for everybody to be able to add to his vernacular one of the urbane languages, French, as his badge of cosmopolitanism. It has worked not too badly.

It is more plausible with manners than with language, our deepest and most useful custom. Gentility manages somehow to appear, if not to shine, in most places, despite the diverse forms which it must manifest. Men apprehend and respond to politeness even when it must disclose itself through esoteric wrappings. American women sometimes appreciate it *because* it comes in strange guise, if one may judge by the marriage of good American commoners to European nobility, whose initial manners are not always eventually fulfilled in wedlock. Yet this preference for the polite is a worthy doorway to the ethical, and the possibility of politeness throughout the world of men marks a path for the universal feasibility of right conduct. Rolling both together, as in nature they make themselves seamless at the junctures, James Russell Lowell, who was himself a man of the world in diplomacy, without ceasing to be a flaming sword of conscience, wrote—

> They are slaves who fear to speak
> For the fallen and the weak.
>
> . . . . . .
>
> They are slaves who dare not be
> In the right with two or three.

Thus Lowell summarizes what we have been saying and paves the way to what must yet be said, in his wise injunction:

> Be noble! and the nobleness that lies
> In other men, sleeping but never dead,
> Will rise in majesty to meet thine own.

DIPLOMACY, GOOD MANNERS AT THE
CORPORATE CROSSROADS

Having said so much, we arrive at the nethermost boundaries of good manners. Two-by-twos men must have the social cement of etiquette, if they are not to generate friction and fall apart. But men must function in collectivities far beyond the domain of love and friendship. Collectivities may be voluntary groupings made up of more or less like-minded individuals possessed of some easy sort of esoteric courtesy, invented to secure and to safeguard like-mindedness. Or they may be made up of larger and less voluntary groupings into which men are born, as they nominally are into churches and necessarily so into states.

Since these latter relations involve unlike-mindedness, as competing churches and as within any given state, the task of implementing mannerliness in them grows more difficult without being less important. Where the state has borrowed from the church the custody of orthodoxy, it also has usually succumbed to the ill-mannerliness of the older sectarianism. There is little hope for political morality where manners sink to the level they did in Italy as Mussolini was rising to power. Mussolini corrupted public taste by using language not as an instrument of communication but as a weapon of assault. Of course he got what he gave: such is the corrupting influence of bad manners. Consider this example from an opposition newspaper, and guess from it what Mussolini had called them.

"Vulgar; indecent; livid; nauseating; insensate; a vagabond in the pay of Jewish societies; pretentious; conscienceless; paranoic; an exalted who madly abandoned himself to the obscene dance of provocation; in the pay of the police; a stupid figure; a ferocious madman; a self-styled Socialist; a rancorous inciter; an unscrupulous liar; a most vile and delinquent sower of hatred; a trickster; a hack writer hardly worth the contempt of gentlemen; a maniac; a criminally lunatic liar; an imbecile; a cretin; and, to boot, a disgusting reptile."

When the democratic state has sunk to such low levels of controversial taste, it has been when religious sectarianism mixed in politics. Nothing that Hamilton, for instance, ever said about his arch-enemy Jefferson could begin to match what the President of Yale College, a divine, publicly said about Jefferson:

For what end shall we be connected with men of whom this is the character and the conduct? Is it that we may assume the same character and pursue the same conduct? Is it that our churches may become temples of reason, our Sabbath a decade, and our psalms of praise Marseillaise Hymns? Is it that we may change our holy worship into a dance of Jacobin phrenzy and that we may behold a strumpet personating a Goddess on the altars of Jehovah? Is it that we may see the Bible cast into a bonfire . . . our wives and daughters the victims of legal prostitution?

In general the modern democratic state is of another mold, and its servants better mannered. They are the soul of gentility in dealing with opponents when action requires assent. It is only the symbol of opposition toward which the politician is generally unmannerly. To the opponent in person, as one can observe in any legislature, mannerliness becomes sheer courtliness. In Congress, for instance, it is seldom the so-and-so from That-Dump-or-This. It is, to the contrary, the "Distinguished Representative from the Land of Cherry, or Apple, or Orange Blossoms—and here's my Best Regards to him, and to the Noble Constituents whom he has the Honor to Represent!" But let us not pursue the collective matter in a manner so individualistic.

Collective "good manners" are known as parliamentary usages. Against the background of English sources, Thomas Jefferson provided our first American manual, and upon his work we have built the marvelous etiquette of our Congress. It would seem theoretically impossible that 435 egoists and orators—The House of Representatives—could when thrown together get any business done. Many people think that they do not get business done; but that is because people look at their representatives when they are in "the thick of thin things." Most of the business of politics *is* to talk, to conduct hearings, to air grievances, to clarify issues, to allay aggressions through the catharsis of vigorous expression. This is mostly the business of parliamentary bodies the world over, not the passing of bills. But when the business is to pass bills, as occasionally it is, there will hardly be found a more efficient body on earth than, say, the American House of Representatives composed of multitudinous members, each eager to exhibit himself and to hear himself. The Rules of the House are so fair and effective that when that body resolves itself into the Committee of the Whole to amend a bill and enact it into law, the business clicks off like cogs perfectly articulated. It is a marvelous achievement, an achievement in nothing more nor less than collective etiquette.

Not ruled out of Congress, but more fully operative elsewhere, is Robert's *Rules of Order,* whereby men—yes, and women, too—are enabled to stop talking all at once, to observe courtesy to one another, and thereby to get transacted whatever collective business may be on hand. The student of ethics who does not see how much we owe to these devices of public procedure has not reached to the roots of morale where conscience painfully compromises itself into the noble thing men call justice. Without public etiquette, not "meetings" but "mobs" would be the order of every day, and collective morale would give way to individual murder, as in the infamous case of Matteoti, which blackened the pages of its record even while fascism, in Italy, was young.

Carl Van Doren, in tribute to Cushing's *Manual of Parliamentary Practice* (1844) and Robert's *Rules of Order* (1876), has spelled these observations out in highly practical form.

"What makes the difference," he asks, "between a meeting and a mob?" He answers in three words: "Rules of order."
But he goes on, if I may briefly excerpt his popular but pungent article, "Two Books We Live By" (*Good Housekeeping*, February 1947):
"A mob has a leader, as a meeting has a chairman; but the leader needs no more than an overbearing will and an overpowering voice. . . . Out of this unthinking unity, this wild stampede, may come actions evil enough to shame mankind and to be regretted bitterly afterward by all but the worst men who had a hand in them."

The lawyers are closest, as a profession, to the generalized courtliness of political manners; they have learned best the difference between meetings and mobs. They have been trained to honor the Court, to respect the opponent, to defer to the jury, and most of all to render homage to the procedure whereby out of a duel in form justice can arise as content. Without such devices—good manners all—utterly impossible would have proved the advances that we celebrate as the democratic fruits of human accommodation.

INTRINSIC REWARDS OF GENTILITY

Our discussion has so far been pitched for the most part upon the level of means. This is the common attitude of those who regard manners as one thing, but morals as another and a better thing. But we who see how the two overlap and how manners help to *constitute* morals, are not fully entitled to the luxury of that distinction. Not only are good manners organic to ethics but they are intrinsic to the life of value. As a current book on manners puts it—*Your Best Foot Forward:*

Among the most important qualities about an individual are, of course, his integrity, his sense of fair play, his regard for the rights of others, his willingness to cooperate with others, his sense of values. It should be remembered, however, that the so-called rules of social usage are built upon these foundations. Respect for the rights of others is the cornerstone upon which social intercourse is built.

Without a doubt Gentility is a good-in-itself. Self-rewarding to watch in practice, it is also self-rewarding to perpetrate. Who does a good thing nobly has done a doubly noble thing. This is the reason why parliamentary politics, simply as a going concern, is the most fascinating, and the most rewarding, enterprise on earth. He who does a mean thing basely has perpetrated a double debasement. This is the reason why mankind will in future ages shudder, or laugh, at the oratorical antics of *Il Duce* of Fascism or at the insane tantrums of *Der Führer* of Nazism. Negative examples apart, let us celebrate the positive. The beautifully done act is beautiful; and among the greatest beauties of life are those personal or institutional values known as good manners.

It was in this spirit, and in pursuance of this very thought, that Plato, the social artist, crowned the dynamics of institutionalization with the garland of enhanced beauty. For passing beyond the comely body and beyond even the noble mind as objects of love, Plato brings us at last, in the dizzy ascent up the ladder of value, to contemplate, as he puts it in the *Symposium,* "the beauty of institutions and laws," until at last through the discipline of an enlarging aesthetics we come face to face with that absolute guerdon of human aspiration, "Beauty itself shining in brightness." All this consummation Plato makes the reward of love, rude enough in the carnal clinches of cave-men, but in him infinitely capable of dialectical purification: a love that can "slow down to kindliness," indeed to political accommodation through patient forbearance and, in our time, through collective compromise.

A FINAL WORD UPON THE PRIVATE AND
THE CRUCIAL

But I would not close on a note, important as it is, so remote from the conscious experience of the student. Politics will teach him good collective manners in due time, if he finds the noble courage to volunteer for its dynamic discipline: to become an agent, that is, of cooperation in areas of unlike-mindedness. There is, however, a growing point of individual morality closer home to the student. It is in the intercourse of friends, and the mastery of a technique to win enemies from enmity. Friendship, like all else that is social and valuable, springs from and thrives upon good manners. Friendship is indeed so dependent upon proper etiquette that it, in self-protection, tends to create that on which alone it naturally feeds. Friendship requires that persons be gentle toward one another, so that minds may meet and spirit be replenished. Between friends speech is never, as so often otherwise it is, either a form of exhibitionism or a mode of assault under cover of communication.

Good manners unlock the door, and they alone will do so, to a reservoir of high and sharable insight. Friendship is so morally fecund that

it, and its conditions, deserve particular emphasis in a book on *Ethics.*
Aristotle was wise in giving such disproportionate space to its discussion.
The wisest men one knows make it a point to talk over with a friend any
action that is ambiguous, before making up their minds as to what they
ought to do. As a moral method, this may appear humble; but it is one
of the most dependable techniques for finding out what is right. It is not
a friend who rushes to settle your affairs for you, with cocksure dogmatism. No, a friend knows enough not even to try "to make such easy simplicity of a life not his own." A friend will listen patiently, his face will
light up or darken; and he may at last open up to think aloud and so
yield perspective that shines like a veritable searchlight upon your quan-
dary. Through his perspective you see for yourself what you had been
overlooking. It is only in such shared intimacy, according to Plato, that
highest truth can gain access to mortal mind—"brought to birth in the
soul on a sudden," so run his matchless words, "as a light that is kindled
by a leaping spark." Operating through such friendship is fulfilled the
famous entity, "Platonic Love." Indeed for this gracious process called
communication Plato elsewhere says, "There is no better helper than
love."

This intimate element in the constitution of the Right has gone into
the making of more greatness than has been recorded by extrovert re-
searchers. But the lyric poets know, know and half reveal in shyness, the
deepest debts of all our hearts. As Jessie Rittenhouse asks,

> For who is he can figure the debt, when all is said,
> Of one who makes you dream again, when all the dreams were dead?

But this moral is written in the triumphs of mind no less than in the
glad despairs of the heart. An excellent American example has indeed
been made of record, and of record luckily in college life: that of Thomas
Jefferson. As a student at William and Mary, Jefferson's gentility (though
he was something of a backwoodsman's son) gained him fortunate access
to the friendship of several men of the world, men whose larger experience became his moral guide in their absence, as in their presences it was
his joy and inspiration.

"Under temptation and difficulties," he later writes of college days, "I would
ask myself what would Dr. Small, Mr. Wythe, Peyton Randolph, do in this
situation . . . knowing the even and dignified line they pursued, I could never
doubt for a moment which of two courses would be in character for them.
Whereas, seeking the same object through a process of moral reasoning, and
with the jaundiced eyes of youth, I should often have erred."

There we have it, the moral method as well as the aesthetic reward which friendship constitutes: ripe fruits both of good manners. This friendship was lucky for the young Jefferson. It is lucky for any young man, or older man or woman, to have these animated prisms, which friends are, to transmute abstract Right into a moral light lustrous enough even to win us to the exacting ways of duty thus disclosed.

Friendship, however—and this is the piercing point of the moral—friendship is not ordinarily a gift of the gods. It is, rather, the culmination of a process the spark-plug of which is good manners, gentle ways, strategic approaches, considerate predispositions. Anybody, but only such a body, can find a friend who himself is friendly. One's "reception," as Lord Chesterfield wrote to his godson, "always depends upon one's behaviour." It is little wonder, with such "reception" as reward for behavior in his youth, that Thomas Jefferson matured so early and so fully as an ethical catalyzer of processes collective. He was at the age of 33 entrusted by patriotic men, their lives thus put at stake, to write for them their Declaration of Independence. He was suffered by fellow-Virginians at the age of 36 to draft, for them to implement, the arduous Statute for Religious Freedom. Living long uncorrupted by power continuously thrust upon him, he founded at the last the great University of Virginia, to institute in connection with it, but off its neutral campus, a system for teaching good manners to those who visibly needed the lesson, even to the self-selected custodians of the morals of others. Behold, what manner of transvaluation of values this is: that a politician, who early against the bitter opposition of sectarians nevertheless saved their freedom from one another's invasion, had late in life to teach the priests and preachers how to be as genteel as the sinners around them. "You may think that Vicars are not usually forgers, and sometimes indeed they are not," slyly insinuates T. H. White in *Mistress Masham's Repose*, "but the heart of man is a strange mechanism . . . and it is astonishing what even Vicars can bring themselves to believe, so long as it is in their own interest."

Thus Jefferson, secular prophet of the Spiritual Life, paved the way to join in distant times the forces of the mannerly with the resources of the "divine," in order to disclose Right and, if it be possible, to make that Right roomy enough for nations, as well as for churches, to live with in peace. Extrapolating the curve of education, Jefferson pointed for our day of the United Nations, as for his less spacious time, the path of our larger national duty: "to suppress passions among ourselves," as he entreats, "and not to blast the confidence we have inspired of proof that a government of reason is better than one of force." That is a vision uplifted of the Right as operative internationally through the mastery of good manners by the nations—beginning, as such charity should begin, at home.

Jefferson was introduced initially as an example of the fecundity for friendship of good manners. His example has expanded naturally to disclose the fruitfulness of such graciousness for statecraft as well. And now, in the growing event, watered by his virtue, let us cite an example which shows Jefferson to have been a consummate practitioner of this virtue under circumstances the most tensional.

John Adams had not only failed of reelection to the Presidency of the United States in 1800 but had disrupted his party in an ill-humored thrust. Alexander Hamilton lashed back at Adams publicly in a most unseemly fashion, and Adams himself was chronically ill-behaved toward colleagues and associates.

When Jefferson came to be inaugurated President, in 1801, he debated with himself whether he should call upon his departing predecessor, John Adams. Deserted as Adams was by his party, devoid of friends, he was sulking his last official hours out in hurt pride. Jefferson feared that Adams would misinterpret his call as a final humiliation; but, like all good-mannered men, the Virginian resolved his doubt on the side of courtesy, preferring to take his risks than to become party to pusillanimity. So he called. Adams did not so much as offer him a chair, but burst out upon sight of his successor: "You have turned me out; you have turned me out!"

"I have not turned you out, Mr. Adams," began Jefferson gently; "and I am glad to avail myself of this occasion to show that I have not and to explain my views. . . . If you and myself had been inexistent, or for any cause had not been selected, other persons would have been selected in our places; and thus the contest would have been carried on, and with the same result, except that the party which supported you would have been defeated by a greater majority, as it was known that, but for you, your party would have carried their unpopular measures much further than they did."

Mollified, Adams offered Jefferson a chair, they talked over old times, and parted with shared feelings of respect. Such examples are not mere good manners; they are the stuff of which institutions, great and solid, get built. The fact that Jefferson and Hamilton did not liquidate each other, when each had his chance, made our American two-party system possible by early providing good sportsmanship to support it. Jefferson and Adams, as all the world knows, became in old age the friends they had been in the stirring days of their early manhood. Their exchange of letters cast a lovely light over their declining years and has left a golden

glow over the nation which they both labored to build. In ethical deference to Jefferson's mannerliness we may now garland the brow of this
Sage of Monticello with the befitting Taoist saying: "The sage antici-
pates things that are difficult while they are easy, and does things that
would become great while they are small."

That is the core of the mannerly which informs the practice of rightness. The Right is clearly the Mannerly, the mannerly and more.

CHAPTER 2

THE RIGHT AS THE LEGAL

If the moralist has a gold mine in the mannerly, from which much of the lustre of his enterprise derives, then in the legal he has found his uranium, from which comes the quintessence of his power. I speak of "power" advisedly; for of the various sources of rightness here alone is concentrated the full might of the community. Gossip makes good manners something not too lightly to be disesteemed as an aspect of the right. Conscience, as we shall see, is morally impressive. But it is the law, as the great Holmes has said, that "is the witness and external deposit of our moral life."

It is in the law indeed we meet at last, and meet for the first time, "here in the law," energy enough to make the right respected by even the mean. You will not understand the law, as Justice Holmes warns, until you catch the slant of the bad man upon it. Here is the form of rightness that can actually be enforced. The fact, however, that not even the legal, no legal, can be one hundred per cent enforced warns us rightly at the outset that we have not yet, not in law, the whole remaining story of morality. Something even here is left to aspiration. But the robust fact that law can be enforced farther than any other form of the right lets us know that our present location is toward the center.

THE LEGAL IS THE ENFORCEABLE RIGHT

Law is the moral mobilized for collective action. The mannerly prevails only so long as not questioned, and the conscientious holds only for the sincere. But the legal can stand doubt, can weather interrogation, can endure cynicism, and still be effective. Neither ignorance, nor doubt, nor dissent is proper defense before the law. Law is not, however, something enforceable over and above the right, though unjust laws can often limp along, effective enough to make citizens miserable. The legal is enforceable, in general, however, not as might but as the collectively accepted right. Not ethically tangential, not subsidiary, not surplus, the law is central to right; for it is the maximum of the right which all, or most, private consciences in any community are able to agree upon.

To see why this is so will yield the moralist something for keeps. Private consciences agree upon the legal as the minimum of what is right because no one of them has any way of getting its convictions accepted as defining the maximum. Better something, however little, than nothing, however high-sounding. Conscience as private insight is precious in the sense that its value may well be limited to the possessor. It may be a little thing, but it is the possessor's very own. To others it may be a piteous thing, because they have their own form of the precious in turn. The maximum becomes the minimum to keep from being nothing.

EVEN TYRANNICAL LAW OFFERS SOME BASIS FOR RIGHTS

Such evaluations hold more or less without regard to the type of law that is involved. Let us begin with law at its worst. Take the ukase of the tyrant: Hitler, let us say, or Mussolini. The command of a superior, even if he is only superior in crass force, gives a basis for common action, to the extent that it can become binding on all subjects. Out of motives of personal convenience, if there be nothing more important, the tyrant can make his will widely binding. He requires order for his own ends, and in the interstices of the seamy order which he gets through decree, subjects will find some security for their ends. So law at its most arbitrary yields what, in its absence, all men would yearn for as a minimal meaning of the right, because a minimal determinant of "rights." To know what to expect, even if it be not of the best, is the beginning of moral wisdom. Hobbes is right: anything is preferable to an anarchic "state of nature." It is law, and law alone, which saves us from that alternative.

This is in fact the motivation on which law has passed from what was more or less arbitrary and less or more cruel and unfair to forms of the right which warrant our warmer praise. Skipping intermediate stages, for we are not trying to write a history of law, we can see how what contained the minimal moral comes to contain the maximum of the moral which men can agree to enforce against one another.

DEMOCRATIC LAW OFFERS WIDE BASIS FOR RIGHTS

When government itself rests upon the consent of the governed, then law, made and re-made by processes of cumulative consent, comes to represent not merely the minimum of the enforceable but gestures toward the maximum of what is publicly right. So long as "rights" themselves are Right (and this must generally be so, or "rights" get dissipated through insecurity), the enforcement of law, to which men consent because they already assented to its being, represents a concrete and enlarging domain of the moral.

Thinking now for simplicity's sake of the Roman Civil and the British Common Law (our two chief American sources of the legal), we can see what a treasure-house of the ethical we have in this double inheritance. There are three large moral functions performed by law: it warns (1) against acts of wrongful injury (*torts,* where private persons are concerned, and *criminal law,* where the public interest is openly involved); it arranges (2) for distribution of deserved benefits (*contracts, property,* etc.); and it provides (3) remedies for injustices that arise either in assessing of penalties or in the distribution of benefits (*procedural* law). The first function of law enables us authoritatively to distinguish liberty from license, and to discourage license; the second teaches us how to effect justice with security; and the third prompts us to rectify excesses and to correct defects in both procedures.

THE LEGAL IS A SUBSTANTIAL PART OF THE MORAL

It was the far range of this potency of law, and its immediate relevance to individual conscience, that led Thomas Hobbes to describe the law "as the public conscience." Hobbes did so out of fear of private conscience, and so he emphasized *public* conscience from disdain for the disorders he saw all around him born of contradictory duties prescribed by sectaries at war with one another. We recognize the validity, and even the positive value, of this insight of Hobbes. But living ourselves in more tolerant and so happier times, we can justly point with pride, even as he viewed with just alarm, to the role of the private conscience in social processes. We can do it all the better when we are discussing law, which in every age tends to level out the eccentricities of private convictions, thus saving conscience from itself.

With us, then, law is not the nemesis of private conscience; it is indeed the fulfillment of it. The good man finds it salutary as well as easy to obey the law. It is true that if the good man merely stays within the law, he is not as good as he might well be. But that means only that the law never embodied all of conscience; it need not mean that its substantial body is not of conscience. It is reassuring that conscience has found a way of getting any of itself publicly fulfilled. There have been times when duties that different private consciences asserted were of such contradictory natures, and of such lethal impetuosity, that men agreed upon little that was infected with common conscientiousness, unless we should count as a wry case of commonalty that they agreed that each ought to jail or kill the other.

Now, however, the good man can say: "I wish the law had gone further, but I subscribe to all that the law requires; and subscribing to its limitations upon others, I submit myself gladly to its exactions." This is not only possible; this is standard procedure in societies where law is the precipitate of popular processes. Such law is moral at a high level and ethical to its center. Not only is it a product of mutual consent; the consent itself is conscience-born and conscience-projected.

Lucky for morality and fortunate for democracy that so much of our legal can be counted as pure contribution to the rightful.

PROCEDURALLY THE ETHICAL CASE GROWS
STRONGER FOR THE LEGAL

So far we have been putting the case at only its moderate strength. A much stronger presentation can be made for the legal as a substantial sector of the moral when we turn to a fuller account of the several agencies through which the legal arises, functions, and grows. We have spoken so far only of the law-giver, whether tyrant or parliament. We have now to speak of the law-maker, including all who interpret the law and all who enforce it. For as in legislation law gets shaped, so in these subsequent processes law gets re-shaped, tempered, refined closer to the pattern of conscience.

To an extent beyond which one sees in the courtroom, however, indeed far beyond this extent, the lawyer as a professional man is the "peacemaker" of the Christian Beatitude. Truth to tell, an overwhelming proportion of the conflicts with which he deals never see the full light of day. (An eminent practitioner has estimated to me that more than ninety per cent of his cases are settled out of court.) Be the percentage what it may, it is the business of the lawyer to settle privately whatever has not got so involved that it must be submitted to the public ordeal of trial.

Most of the work of the legal profession, foresworn as it is to constructive ideals, is the drawing up of agreements, trusts, contracts in language so clear that conflicts (over interpretation as well as substance) will not in the future arise to trouble the consciences of good citizens, and to ruffle the peace of the community.

When conflicts come to this latter pass, however, the student must see what a moral advantage even court procedure has over its only alternatives, i.e., settlement by duel, usurpation by the stronger, or vendetta. Beyond the obvious and the noisy, is this mighty and quiet work of the law in the interest of social harmony. But it is in crisis that one sees at its most crucial the creative aspect of the legal profession. There is a conservative, or even progressive, morality, which merely carries on. There is also a dynamic, or even radical, ethics, which supervenes collectively to resolve conflicts, otherwise morally lethal, when conscience gets set against conscience and group digs in against group for the duration. This latter constitutes the moral challenge which leads up to legislation through politics and down from legislation through administration and adjudication, where participate some or all of the trinity of this good work: judge, lawyers, jury.

If in a government of laws the total process were left merely to the moralist, the legal results would be morally worse than they are. The moralist is ordinarily only a speculator, with the blue sky as his limit. He is likely to disdain the earth, since the upper air is freer and purer. The moralist usually knows little enough about the earth anyhow; and it may be that he knows no more about the sky. At the level of the empyrean it is harder to expose his ignorance. On earth, it is easy enough, from experience, to see that no narrow inexperience can be trusted to discern wisdom of policy. Unmortgaged to the best custom and irresponsive to law, most moralists would as law-givers reveal themselves as the sheer theorists they are. *Would? Do,* as a matter of fact.

AN OBJECT LESSON OF UTOPISTS

Utopias are the clothed skeletons of what, when seen naked, are not sights to look upon with ease. Plato's *Republic* is the Greek's notion of moral goodness writ large in public policy; but a more tyrannical and impossible place for a free man to live has hardly been conceived, certainly not short of a concentration camp. Mr. George Santayana has properly taken the number of Plato's error in *Platonism and the Spiritual Life.* I shall here only glance at the skeletons in the morgue.

Why, Plato sets himself to censoring the deity, to expurgating the scriptures, banishing atheists and re-writing poetry, after kicking certain kinds of artists out altogether. We pass in charity his communism of women and children, out of deference to Lenin's earthly restraint, as compared with Plato. Apart from the immorality of Plato's moral paradise, it is, what is almost harder to forgive, so infernally monotonous. Indeed, this trait at least appears common to all the major utopias. An American should be examined by a psychiatrist who would elect to live in More's *Utopia,* Butler's *Erewhon,* or Harrington's *Oceana* (to take only three other well known ones).

It is the beginning of wisdom for the moralist (Everyman, I mean), and a plug for law, to discover that the moralist unhampered cannot build a paradise that will wear as well as the old trial-and-error societies that mankind has already blundered into cooperatively, right here on earth. Let the young idealist ponder deeply this thought. For the essence of the wisdom is the discovery that men want variety as well as require uniformity. This necessity for variety, for even extemporized variety, is what is easiest for the moralist to forget. Forgetting it, he builds his utopias on molds of uniformity more severe than he himself could stomach as steady fare.

America has been fortunate in early and continuing clairvoyance of this necessity of variety. The colonists learned before the Revolutionary War, learned it the hard way from one another, that it is better to have no church than to have only one church, though every church strove at first to be the one and only. John Cotton, the Puritan, taught what Roger Williams, the independent, could never forget; and Roger Williams memorialized the sad lesson. Thomas Jefferson learned the hard way, too, that the only recourse, to save piety from the poison of power, was to pluralize the power which piety claims. Not only in practice, through his Virginia Statute for religious freedom, but in theory immortally phrased, Jefferson sent ringing down the American ages what utopists of every age have forgotten, the factual necessity as well as the moral desirability of variety in both institutions and the conscientious convictions of men.

In his *Notes On Virginia* he records the conviction of variety in a manner unique to him and culturally befitting the century of tolerance in which he lived. He had travelled widely and sympathized deeply with all sorts of men. So facing up to the theoretical issue, he asks very pointedly: "Is uniformity attainable? Millions of innocent men, women and children, since the introduction of Christianity, have been burnt, tortured, fined, imprisoned; yet we have not advanced one inch toward uniformity. What has been the effect of coercion? To make one half the world fools, and the other half hypocrites. To support roguery and error all over the earth." From this he concludes, in the same work, that "difference of opinion is advantageous in religion. The several sects perform the office of a *censor morum* over each other."

To a friend he writes: "The varieties in structure and action of the human mind as in those of the body, are the work of the Creator, against which it cannot be a religious duty to erect the standard of uniformity." And, finally, in making it possible for all sects to have representation at his own University of Virginia, not on but off the campus (a pattern still followed in many American universities), Jefferson explained his strategy as not the cynical one "to divide and conquer" but as the humane one to scatter the poison of power and thus to purify piety: "And by bringing the sects together, and mixing them with the mass of other students, we shall soften their asperities, liberalize and neutralize their prejudices, and make the general religion a religion of peace, reason, and morality."

What our Fathers learned from the bitter experience of religious persecution and what Jefferson memorialized for them, this it was that was written into our Bill of Rights so that the variety which is natural in religion and unavoidable throughout man's inner life should never be interfered with artificially. This clairvoyance has achieved its proper voice in every succeeding generation, in spite of constant attrition against it by sectaries pushing for power in the name of some particular brand of piety. The latest voice, coming as it does from Mr. Justice Jackson on the Supreme Court, reaffirms as ringingly as Jefferson's, the odiousness of enforced uniformity and the beauty and fertility of efflorescent variety. "As governmental pressure for unity becomes greater," says the Justice, and it is worth repeating,

"so strife becomes more bitter as to whose unity it shall be. . . . Those who begin coercive elimination of dissent soon find themselves exterminating dissenters. Compulsory unification of opinion achieves only the unanimity of the graveyard. . . . If there is any fixed star in our constitutional constellation, it is that no official, high or petty, can prescribe what shall be orthodox in politics, nationalism, religion, or other matters of opinion, or force citizens to confess by word, or act their faith therein."

These citations bring us back to home base in considering the Right as the legal. Laws are not finished when they leave the hands of dictators or achieve formulation by parliaments. Newborn statutes are but lusty candidates for legality; they must yet run the gamut of concrete implementation. Courts have, and have always had, a hand in fashioning the legal. Legality profits greatly in rightness from the fact. The judge is learned in precedent. He has his feet in the soil of the customary. His head cannot soar beyond the precedential without a warning buzz of judicial dizziness. He acts only upon specific cases, though upon these he acts in the light of the general. He thus combines theory and practice, to the moral purification of both.

The judge is, moreover, flanked by lawyers, who bring to questions of procedure the steady light of a learned craft. Good manners yield through them what custom offers in the judge's respect for precedent. Moreover, intelligence is sharpened by the form of a duel, in which opposing counsel leave no resource of ingenuity untried to budge the judge this way or that. Custom is dented by intelligence; ingenuity is bent back by custom. Mr. Justice Jackson has paid this tribute to the American lawyers, especially the country lawyers of the 19th century: "Paper 'rights' are worth, when they are threatened, just what some lawyer makes them worth. Civil liberties are those which some lawyer, respected by his neighbors, will stand up to defend. Any legal doctrine which fails to enlist the support of well-regarded lawyers will have no real sway in this country."

And, touchstone of all, is the jury, present in symbol when absent in fact. It is the symbol of commonsense, of popular participation in learned processes, of widely shared consent. The whole judicial (and in our time much of the administrative) process must meet the acid test of criticism from those who are affected by decisions. If the jury is present, they are the laymen who in mundane sanity mediate the learning of the judge and the technicalities of the learned profession of the lawyers. Fact is always a fair, if severe, test for theory, and social consent to justice is the continuing form of purification without which no man knows whether he is in the main stream or not.

Whoever surveys the elements that go into the legislative and that come out of the judicial processes for the determination in concrete cases of what is right—and still thinks that he, with unaided intuition, prompted only by conscience, can justly have the moral skip the legal—he is a god or a fool.

LAW-MAKER VERSUS LAW-GIVER

Since we cannot be gods, not yet, let us take counsel how not to be fools. Civilized peoples make themselves fools when they succumb to the Communistic propaganda to the effect that politics must be banished before men can be happy. Wise men know that if and when politics *withers away,* as is promised in the gospel according to St. Marx, politicians will still be in the saddle with this sad disadvantage as compared with now: there will then be no recourse against them. Politics we must have as the instrument of a growing morality. The choice, then, is this: self-elected politicians who cannot be unseated even when known to be rascals, or politicians elected who can be unseated upon even the suspicion of injustice. The ancients talked of law-givers because they thought of law as *given,* needing only to be distributed to the people by its wise discoverers and proud possessors. Moderns talk of law-makers because moderns think—and it is a thought most sedate—of law not as pre-existent to be discovered by the self-nominated wise, but of law as outgrowth of individual experiences pooled to precipitate rules of the game acceptable to all.

It is much easier to talk of pooling than it is to pool anything, and especially to pool experience which is divergent and is reinforced in its divergence by consciences that have already jelled, so to say. Two-party politics represents the best that we have found out about this process of pooling. What we can pool, that only can we make into law. The sad thing about democracy—it is sadder still about autocracy—is that much that is finest is lost in the process of cooking and canning: the compromises, i.e., of equally honorable but downright divergent notions of justice. To understand how that is and why it must be so, is final preparation for accepting the legal as right; indeed for accepting a certain kind of legal as *the* right for the situation that both necessitates and legitimizes laws.

POLITICS THE ALMA MATER OF THE MORAL

The political process is by innocents often set over against the moral process. And there is just here a paradox which requires more than innocence to resolve. Out of political compromise there does come only the minimum, as we have been saying, of what private consciences previously regarded as right. But the reason for the minimum is not what innocents think, not that politics is "rotten" or that politicians are dishonest. The reason is different and deeper: it is that good men insist upon being good in such divergent ways, each (at least each group) in his *own* way, calling *this* way, *the* way.

Collective experience indeed suggests that the more intelligent men are the more they will differ on things important (like religion, for instance) and the more honest they are, the more they will set store upon their differences. At any rate it is a fact observable, and by the weak deplored, that honest men differ on honesty, just men quarrel over justice, and good men dispute over the ownership of goods. In such situations, morality ceases to operate simply. It tends to turn into its opposite. The Right is dissipated by a diversity of claimants, each self-nominated to monopolize in the end (in the beginning to monopolize the interpretation of) what both sides claim.

Supervening upon such a (chronic) predicament democratic politics becomes a moral method (the only one short of the worse one, dictatorship) for precipitating a minimum of Right out of the self-suicide of Right through the conflict of monopolistic claims. Politics becomes thus the mother of morality in the dark night of collective parturition. A child is born, bald, misshapen, and noisy, but he is later christened Justice —and not infrequently lives to honor his name. This is law, democratic law, and this is the way in which the crossroads of morality become the roadbed of the legal, and the manner in which the legal in turn becomes the highroad of morality.

As compensation for any defects in this legal pathway to the moral, we have in it a *growing* right. Politics of this variety is a self-renewing and self-corrective process. It mediates unlike-mindedness, and brings to birth continuously the fruits of peace in a context martial. The process is a high achievement, and the product is mankind's most standard definition of the reasonable.

If you would know what is right, look then to the law; for the legal is the moral: always in part, frequently in large part, sometimes in crucial part. Never forget the legal when questing for the Right.

Let us then reaffirm that the Right is the legal, the legal and more.

CHAPTER 3

THE RIGHT AS THE NATURAL

No moralist is well advised to avert his eyes from the spontaneous prompt-ings that recur from age to age in the opinions of plain people and that get continuously echoed by the poets and grounded in the aphorisms of mankind. To this caution we have heretofore paid systematic heed, and to it we must now pay further attention if we are not to neglect a guid-ance toward which common sense always prompts. We cannot ignore, nor have we tried to depreciate, the deference men pay manners. The legal is everywhere visible to remind us of the rigid framework of morality. Similarly, men repair in every age and under all conditions to the notion that what is "natural" is somehow right.

Let us admit to begin with, however, that "Nature" is more ambiguous than any norm thus far considered. For every Milton to caution us—

> Accuse not Nature, she hath done her part;
> Do thou but thine—

and for every Wordsworth to invite us—

> Come forth into the light of things,
> Let Nature be your teacher—

there is a Thomas Hood to insinuate that

> . . . the book of Nature
> Getteth short of leaves;

and there is an Alfred Tennyson to bemoan a

> Nature red in tooth and claw,

and, above all, a Thomas Hobbes to indict:

> It may seem strange . . . that Nature should thus dissociate,
> and render men apt to invade, and destroy one another . . .
> a life poor, nasty, brutish, and short.

This latter note, of deep discordance, had best be attended to at once, lest it poison our positive intent. Every student of philosophy knows how easy it is to make fun of the ambiguity of this concept of *Nature;* but he also knows, or should now learn, that what survives all ridicule may have more to it than the ridiculous. Hobbes has furnished the immortal indictment, in a passage following the one which we have just quoted from the *Leviathan.* He invites us to consider a series of events and asks us to answer *why* to each event: why man "when taking a journey, arms himself, and seeks to go well accompanied; when going to sleep, locks his doors; when even in his house locks his chests; and then when he knows there be laws, and public officers, armed, to revenge all injuries shall be done him; what opinion he has of his fellow subjects, when he rides armed; children, and servants, when he locks his chests. Does he not there as much accuse mankind by his actions, as I do by my words?"

Yet Hobbes concludes his deprecatory interrogations with a distinction that opens the door to a better understanding of the moral rendition proper to the 'natural' as norm. Speaking of his critics and of himself together, Hobbes says, "But neither of us accuse man's nature in it. The desires, and other passions of man, are in themselves no sin. No more are the actions that proceed from those passions, till they know a law that forbids them." These latter words betoken a detour into Hobbes' own political authoritarianism intended by him as desperate repair work for the deplorable state of man. We shall not now be diverted to that detour. But the proffered diversion does suggest that for every weakness there is a defense. We shall ourselves, the rather, pursue the lead opened by Hobbes in his distinction between 'Nature' and human nature. This distinction does not always lead to such an easy method as Wordsworth's "wise passiveness" nor to so rapturous an eventuation as this poet's moral rhapsody in green—

> One impulse from a vernal wood
> 　May teach you more of man,
> Of moral evil and of good
> 　Than all the sages can.

But the distinction will lead us along a solid historic trail through Stoic materialism to a background glance at Heraclitean rationalism, then, forward, through primitive Christianity to the ageless and sectless "divine," through deterministic Spinozism to roseate pantheism, through Bishop

Butler inward to conscience, informed of deity, and through the romantic poets to a cosmic harmony, in which man's

> . . . glories float between the earth and heaven
> Like clouds which seem pavilions of the sun.

Out of love for the poets* and with deference to the philosophers and divines, let us now seek to distil from these several sources in historic turn all the aid we can get in our quest for the moral as the natural. No definition here, least of all here, will wholly contain what is defined, because of the generous plethora of interpretations already suggested. But we shall emerge with substance for wiser living for having listened to the voices of Nature constituting as they do a "various language"—

> . . . Powers
> Which of themselves our minds impress;
> That we can feed this mind of ours
> In a wise passiveness.

We shall also disclose and confirm an intellectual strategy from which we have already been, more or less unconsciously, profiting. As touching this strategy, we shall see how this philosophy of the 'natural,' like every moral philosophy but more visibly and modestly than most, buttresses its flanks against attack by borrowing aid from its allies, the other schools of moral philosophy. However simple our doctrine at the start, the notion of nature as moral norm becomes in the event a genuinely synthetic philosophy, *e pluribus unum*. Through the historic meanderings of this one theory we shall see how each philosophy may, as each should, borrow from all to the profit of each and the honor of all.

A PARADOX AND ITS LESSON

It was Stoicism that first formulated the promptings of nature into a doctrine. Remembering how austere Stoicism sounds, the student will get an inkling of what is to follow, and it is what he always needs to be learning lest the agility of the philosophic mind lead him away from wisdom toward cynicism, that Nemesis of all who drink too lightly of the Pierian spring. If to live naturally means, as in Rousseau, for instance, to take it easy, to surrender to emotional openings as they arise, the "nature" in-

---

* Our differential attention paid in this chapter to the poets is, on the defense, an open acknowledgment of the ambivalence, yea the ambiguity, of this rendition of the Right; but it is no less, on the offense, a patient reaffirmation of confidence that moral guidance is where men find their guides. Nature is as a matter of fact one such guide. Age has not withered, not yet, nor custom staled, still not yet, man's affinity with his common mother.

volved ought to have become the mainstay of Epicureanism, the pleasure path of life: as Tennyson has it—

> Sensations sweet,
> Felt in the blood, and felt along the heart.

Stoicism should, on the other side, have expressed itself in some austere formulation connoting the abstention for which it popularly stands. To the contrary, Epicureanism, taking pleasure as norm, prescribes as rule what Socrates calls the "art of mensuration," which becomes the "saving principle of life." Neat pleasures are dangerous preferences; only *calculated* pleasures are dependable risks for a prudent man. This begins to sound not easy but hard. The whole history of hedonism illustrates this reversion, until in Utilitarianism morality achieves its rationality in what Jeremy Bentham calls the "felicific calculus," which takes a wise man— and an adding machine—to operate effectively.

This is but to say, on the one side, that every moral theory is both a thrust and a defense. The defense, to be effective, must be of weaknesses disclosed in if not caused by the thrusting. Every moral postulation is a sort of Battle of the Bulge, woe betiding any little Hitler who 'bulges' without circumspect regard for his rear and both his flanks. Some impulsive Patton lies in wait to fall upon Consistency advancing beyond its logical lair. As Goethe sings it,

> Grau, teurer Freund, ist alle Theorie,
> Und grün des Lebens goldener Baum.

The caution that attends hedonism is a necessary part of any circumspect philosophy. Its extreme is stated in the hedonistic paradox: "to get pleasure, we must indeed forget it!" It is this type of defended thrust which we shall see in further developing Stoicism's "live according to nature" doctrine. This philosophy is a defense not against rigor, as appears, but against laxity, as we shall soon see. *Nature* prescribes no easy way; she is but prostituted by agents of ease, who bring her into disrepute. Hers is a way so hard that Stoicism has become the epitome of austerity, in spite of its easy-sounding symbol.

Truth to tell, the historic appeal to Nature for moral guidance has done more to 'nature' than it has to man, if we may so phrase the matter. Nature indeed becomes *human* nature, as in the previous insinuation from Hobbes, and that in turn gets best exemplification in the superhuman Sage or the supernatural Saint. "Life according to nature" came quickly in Heraclitus, to exploit "fire" as somehow constitutive of nature and basic to human nature. The flame that quickens us individually as soul, this flame is not unakin to the fire that burns at the heart of the universe. Dissolving all else through analysis, building up whatever it may through synthesis, this fire takes the form of bright-glowing, leaping Reason. "To live according to nature" meant, then, to a Stoic to cut through the spaciousness of illusion and to pierce to the heart of the matter, to the cosmically purifying role of rationality itself. Since reason is cosmic and man is alive with it, the universe is friendly to man, its spiritual manikin. Man needs only to understand in order to find his comfort in this all-engulfing affinity. "If it were according to nature," says Aurelius with complete piety, "nature would have it so." So conceived, the cosmos becomes Providence, in which man lives and loves and has his harmonious being. Says Aurelius again, "Thou must neither blame chance nor accuse Providence." Man's freedom is to be at one with his environment, to be determined by it, and to accept the determination with equanimity of spirit. The Stoics were complete determinists, needing no other freedom than humble acknowledgment of complete dependence.

Men who see reality thus will not think themselves privileged to stand outside and to complain at the way the world wags. "When thou art troubled about anything," cautions Aurelius, "thou hast forgotten this, that all things happen according to the universal nature." If it is not always to our liking, that is only too bad for our liking. We ought to learn to "like" more rationally. The universe is not in man; it is man who is in the universe. He must not arrogate to himself more of responsibility than he has of power. So the maxim of Epictetus to inquire first what is within one's power and what is without it. What is within one's power, let one order to specification. That is one's privilege. What is beyond one's power, is none of his business. Let him not, therefore, concern himself with it.

Under our control [says Epictetus] are conception, choice, desire, aversion, and, in a word, everything that is our own doing; not under our control are our body, our property, reputation, office, and, in a word, everything that is not our own doing. . . . Remember, therefore, that if what is naturally slavish you think to be free, and what is not your own to be your own, you will be hampered, will grieve, will be in turmoil, and will blame both gods and men; while if you think only what is your own to be your own, and what is not your own to be, as it really is, not your own, then no one will ever be able to exert compulsion upon you, no one will hinder you, you will blame no one, will find fault with no one, will do absolutely nothing against your will, you will have no personal enemy, no one will harm you, for neither is there any harm that can touch you.

Marcus Aurelius, the Emperor, makes common cause with Epictetus, the slave, in this recommendation: "If thou art pained by any external thing, it is not this thing that disturbs thee, but thy judgment about it. And it is in thy power to wipe out this judgment now."

Such natural piety can easily become a religion. Stoicism is indeed the type of religion to which mankind gravitates when the going gets hard. Such an outlook toughens man not to expect more than can be fulfilled, and coaches him in one way, though not our contemporary way, of happiness: to want whatever you get, since you can never get what you want. Of the two standard recipes for happiness—to minimize desire or to maximize goods—the Stoic recommended the former.

In this way Stoicism passed from what sounds too easy to deserve philosophic attention—life merely according to nature—to what proves too hard for ordinary men: obedience to so stern a view of the reasonable as leaves no room for grief, none for repentance, and little for any of the more human sentiments. That there is wisdom, however, in toughening man's fibers, our age has learned the hard way, the rugged way of war. The Stoic way of nature was, then, the hard path of reason, the best guidance human intelligence could provide for the stony high-road of daily life in an age of political decadence.

THE CHRISTIAN MODIFICATION

It is a short step from Nature so conceived, to its being made the eternal fire that is "divine": from cosmic to macrocosmic Reason. The Stoics understood the transition, but took it calmly. "No longer," as one of them said, "Dear City of Cecrops, but now dear City of God." The Gospel according to St. John opens with a passage which spells out the continuity between Stoicism and Christianity and celebrates its joint substance ecstatically: "In the beginning was the Word [the Greek term for Reason, *Logos*], and the Word was with God, and the Word was God." One need find the impersonal world only too cold to be borne (or deity too remote to be invoked) in order to enable him to understand this modification from a sort of pantheistic system all-inclusive to a solicitous creator all-encompassing. In this continuity we may think of Christianity as Stoicism made personal to all, palatable to the weak, rewarding to all the faithful.

The word "nature" in Christianity is variously used. It ranges in meaning from what is customary [St. Paul found long hair "natural" to women, short hair "unnatural," though it is the reverse with men!] to what is genuinely "divine." Since God is lord of nature, nature is a mundane rendition of deity. Disdaining man's elemental impulses and depreciating the world to which they belonged, Christians made life mean to pattern one's action after the will of God. To do this is at least "second nature" and superior nature—"natural" to all who have been "born again." The norm of nature became more favorably viewed in Christian theology as the rationalization tendency leavened piety and as the romanticizing movement did its work upon the world of nature. In between these two tendencies, Thomas Aquinas made "nature" one of the necessary norms of law. "Natural law" became and remains for Roman Catholics the second order of law, being defined by St. Thomas as "nothing less than the rational creature's participation of the eternal law."

This conception of a *natural* prompting in man toward the *supernatural* is indeed common to Protestant and Catholic Christianity. St. Thomas argues for it from a gloss on the famous Pauline text, a text ever popular also with Protestant divines: "when the Gentiles, which have not the law, do by nature the things contained in the law, these, having not the law, are a law unto themselves." The Catholic gloss, as quoted by St. Thomas, reads: "Although they have no written law, yet they have the natural law, whereby each one knows, and is conscious of, what is good and what is evil." For Protestantism, Bishop Butler has given the gloss—a whole sermon's worth—upon the same text, and in general with equal edification. Since we concern ourselves with Butler's insight in the chapter on "The Right as the Conscientious," let us but summarize it here, and attach a moral. The summary is: Conscience is given man as "natural" guide to what revelation yields *super-naturally*. The moral, to remind here again of what we have called the strategy of virtue, is this: the notion that the Right is the "natural" runs into, and borrows from, many theories, notably here from conscience and both through and around conscience from the "divine."

THE SPINOZISTIC COMBINATION

When we recall Roman Stoicism at its uttermost, we are already near to Spinoza's rendition of ethics in modern times. Aurelius had declared that "whatever happens at all happens as it should." And he had made this mean that "even death is one of the things that Nature wills." It is required, then, only to tighten up the bolts a little, so that, with Alexander Pope,

> . . . binding nature fast in fate,
> Let free the human will,

we may find magnificent freedom in making completely clear to ourselves the nature of our bondage, metaphysical and austere. As proper text for exposing his part, let us take Spinoza's saying: "It is impossible for a man not to be a part of nature and not to follow its general order." If at times this inevitability appears ill, it is when, and it is because, human nature is not working to the top of its rational powers. Rationally regarded, as he goes on to say, "There is nothing in nature that is opposed to the understanding; nothing that can destroy it."

That is admittedly a hard saying, but Spinoza does his utmost to make it appear intelligible and inevitable. He does it, primarily, in a book which, though called *Ethics,* will strike the student more like geometry than like morals. This is partly because Spinoza was anxious to tie all things down rigorously as he went, harassing his ideas until after them he could write "Q.E.D." It was his way, in a period when mathematics looked like a new secular technique of infallibility, a method of leaving no cosmic bolts loose. Taking his method for what it is, however, his motivation can plainly be seen to be what men have always called moral or religious. Spinoza, though born a Jew, had been driven from the Synagogue with a terrible curse for beliefs that left his fellow-communicants branding him an atheist but which led men with more discernment to think of him as "a God-intoxicated" man. It was indeed salvation, nothing less, which Spinoza sought, but since the "divine" had been denied him institutionally, he sought the guerdon—"continuous, supreme, and unending happiness"—individually and naturalistically.

The story of his high quest, as suggested by him, is saved from pathos, if you will but have it so, through heroism. Ordinary recourses had failed him. He would not be frustrated, not by any such denial to his soul's ambition. He would have had an institutional God, but the means of grace had been withdrawn, so withdrawn that Spinoza had to seek asylum for his life in non-Jewish residence. Fame had for the season failed him, which he, being human, would have had—but not the easy way. Wealth had failed him, a meagre living from lens-grinding being all that was securely left him, though a small competence from a friend later came to succor him in his pulmonary illness. In short, happiness had failed Spinoza, as happiness is normally reckoned. What though all externalia, including health, were lost, not all was yet lost. There were internal resources. The former were "outside his powers"; and by Stoic doctrine should therefore be dismissed. But what *was* "within the power" of a poor Jew, persecuted by orthodox Jews, despised by many Gentiles?

His mind was still within his power. His mind and its discernments. And what was it that his mind discerned for him? This: that since the universe was a seamless whole, as the scientists were newly proclaiming, the acceptance of its wholeness freed one from anxiety and made him at home, completely at home in his world, as the ancient Stoics had long since declared. Necessity rebelled against, spells misery. Necessity accepted, spells . . . well, according to Spinoza, spells "blessedness."

His favorite word is thus a religious one, for he was in quest of salvation. This was his salvation: natural piety to accept the universe just as it is.

> Fly from pain, and you will find
> Pain forever close behind.
> Make no protest; do not cry;
> Never struggle for release.
> Let it do the worst it can;
> After this comes peace.
>   (JAMIE SEXTON HOLME)

This "peace" of the poet is the "blessedness" of the philosopher. Fate is transmuted into freedom through full acquiescence. Here we are, we and the world: we in the world. The world does something to us; we do something to the world. Let us call what the world does to us "passion," for it spells suffering for us. It is below the full dignity of man, who is a noble part of nature, to allow himself to be victimized by the whole of nature. There is, then, what we do to nature; "activity," let us call it, to distinguish creativeness of an actor from the passivity of a victim. What we do to the world expresses our initiative and symbolizes our vantage. Action is within our power, and the most solvent form of it is thought. Passion is without our power so long as we sit and suffer it. But if we stand and take it, we transmute it in the act of reception. We may, that is, act upon passion; and when we do, passion ceases to be what it was, and becomes what understanding makes it. "An emotion," says Spinoza, "which is a passion, ceases to be a passion as soon as we form a clear and distinct idea thereof."

Thus, even before the psychoanalysts, cosmic defeat is turned into a moral victory by the alchemy of insight—and the heroism of natural piety. It is proper to speak of heroism, for this acceptance must be large, as large as God [the sum-total of things], and it must be loving as well as large. Combining these, Spinoza indeed calls the act and attitude which together yield salvation, "the intellectual love of God." Such blessedness "is not the reward of virtue, but virtue itself." Having discovered, or thought to discover, that the scientist is the best theologian if he but feed upon large as well as local causes, Spinoza closes his *Ethics* upon a note of triumph. "It is evident," begins he in summarizing his discovery, "how much stronger and better the wise man is than the ignorant man, who is held by mere desire. For the ignorant man, besides being agitated in many ways by external causes has never attained true satisfaction of the soul, lives as it were without consciousness of himself, of God, and of things, and just as soon as he ceases to be acted upon, ceases to be. While on the contrary the wise man is little disturbed in mind, but conscious by a certain eternal necessity of himself, of God, and of things, he never ceases to be, but is always possessed of true satisfaction of soul." And then with a touch of apology, redeemed by noble pride, Spinoza concludes: "If indeed, the path that I have shown to lead to this appear difficult, yet it may be found, and all excellent things are as difficult as they are rare."

A FINAL WORD FOR NATURE

Such, then, though it appear a far cry, is the case for the "natural" as one meaning of the Right. Epictetus—and who more than he deserved the consolation?—declared: "If you live according to nature, you will never be poor." Poor as Spinoza was, he was through this spirit immortally enriched; and all who knew him bore witness to the magnanimity of his nature. There is much to be said for taking Nature as our guide. She grows under a regime of confidence in her, grows and grows until the man is lucky who, architect of his own fate, "serves Nature, knows Nature, is Nature," as Philip Wylie says in his *Essay on Morals*. Such a man is lucky because, as Wylie concludes, "all Nature serves him when he so is and acts." Thinking also of the artist in man, Ralph Waldo Emerson similarly appraises the role of the man who listens in upon the lucid voices of nature:

> He who overhears some random word they say,
> Is the fated man of men whom the ages must obey.

If the ages "must obey" such a man, the necessity arises from a law of their own nature, a law that prescribes spontaneity as the condition of human excellence. This is the final wisdom of the norm of nature: that the best arises only from "naturalness"—lack of self-consciousness. To minimize self-consciousness while maximizing consciousness itself, this is a sober maxim which all reflection seems to reinforce.

In everything which we have considered, the paradox returns to haunt us: *to get . . . forget . . .* As a late manual on etiquette says, "To be always thinking about your manners is not the best way to make them good." "Be natural, always," another manual declares, "and you will have the most chance of being popular." From manners to morals (though, as we have shown, it is not the jump men think), Goethe, commenting upon an attitude he thought squeamish declared: "It shows a too tender

conscience. . . . Such a conscience makes hypochondriacal men, if it is
not balanced by great activity." This "o'er-sickling" of things with the
"pale cast of thought" must be *worked off,* that is, if it is not to impair
the end which it aspires to gain.

Right is somehow the proper response of man to the proper object;
and, as to what is meant by "proper," spontaneity, while not an absolute
guarantee, is certainly the test close at hand. This seems the underlying
reason—and if so, an adequate reason—for man's return in every age to
the "natural" as a promising pathway to the Right.

The Right is the Natural, the natural and more.

CHAPTER 4

THE RIGHT AS THE CONSCIENTIOUS

It is universally believed that Right is defined in some part by what is conscientious. In large part, for most men. And, on the negative side, altogether for all civilized men. Henry Sidgwick, author in nineteenth century England of the frequently quoted *Methods of Ethics,* expressed a conclusion from which there could hardly be found a dissent in the civilized world, that "no act can be absolutely right, whatever its external aspect and relations, which is believed by the agent to be wrong." It does not follow, on the positive side, however, that a conscientious act must always and ever be necessarily right. That is quite another question, a question so open as to make glad room for all honest methods of finding the Right. Circumspectly put, *an unconscientious act can never be right but a conscientious one can sometimes be wrong.*

CONSCIENCE AND SUBJECTIVE RIGHTNESS

The reason for the distinction, a reason which shows the distinction to be necessary for the good of all, is that there is an inner aspect to every conscious act, and no act could be "subjectively" right that was not believed to be right, whereas it might be "objectively" wrong, whatever the attitude be of him who does it. So deep in us lies the wisdom of both internal acceptance and external caution that we have aphorisms that tend to cancel each other out. We say, as corrective of narrow-visored motives, that "the road to hell is paved with good intentions." But we also "take the will for the deed." We say, as corrective of the conceit of a hard-boiled extroversion, that "the pure in heart shall see God," or of excessive worldly wisdom that "a little child shall lead them." But we also say that "God helps those who help themselves." The double truth is that we dare not wholly ignore motives, for out of them proceed consequences; and we dare not be cavalier about consequences, for motives get corrected only by reference to them, in the penance of hindsight if not through the caution of foresight.

No concern over this ambivalence, however, can obscure from us the importance of conscience as one of mankind's oldest guides to the Right. Nor has this insight been left without its witnesses in chapters that have gone before this one. Out of conscience arises, through such processes of agreement as any political season affords, most of what constitutes democratic law, and much that passes for any kind of law. Moreover, it is the channel, almost the standardized channel, through which the "divine" is funnelled into daily accessibility. And we shall presently behold conscience arising from a baptism in Reason as the humble *alter ego* of Kant's Categorical Imperative. This is praise enough for conscience on any weekday, and praise of it on Sunday entails equivocal consequences, as we shall soon see. Only good manners are left out of our résumé. They are omitted because conscience usually disdains them, to its own hurt.

Actually, conscience is the common man's synonym for what is right. The "voice" which spoke to Socrates, telling him what not to do, was conscience, the selfsame voice which speaks to common men today. The "voice" to which St. Paul harkened when others with him heard nothing, was conscience, the very voice that stops sensitive men today from similar sadism. The "other man" within, to which Gandhi showed deference, was conscience, the same voice that makes humane men hesitant about using force today. The "still small voice" of Everyman, that is always and everywhere conscience. If we go by hunches, we call that guidance good luck. If we attend to argument, that is persuasion. If we calculate our conduct, that is prudence. If we figure our perplexity out, that is ingenuity. If we reason ourselves out of a hole, that is scientific intelligence. But if we consult the monitor within, that is the guidance of conscience. As Shakespeare in King Henry VIII characterizes this climax:

> "A peace above all earthly dignities,
> A still and quiet conscience."

George Washington wrote in his school-boy copy-book the maxim:

> "Labor to keep alive in your breast
> the little spark of celestial fire, Conscience."

CONSCIENCE AS COMPANION OF THE EARTHY

Since we are to set the Categorical Imperative apart for special treatment, we here do well to identify the systematic claims of conscience with a moralist less austere, though not less sincere nor less significant, than Immanuel Kant. I refer to Bishop Butler, an Anglican 18th-century divine whose sermons were ethical treatises. He has raised a powerful voice, within the Anglo-Saxon tradition, on behalf of conscience as guide to right. The Bishop could, as a professional Divine, have fallen back on Revelation. For an honor to God less esoteric, however, he found in conscience, or hoped to find, a nearer and more certain guide to right conduct than the voice of deity dispatched to him neatly. In his powerful moral homily on the Pauline text that "the Gentiles which have not the divine law . . . are a moral law unto themselves," Butler seeks to distinguish conscience from both revelation and impulse and so to free it from both church and the world. He shows, on the one side, or seeks to show, that God, in the wisdom of his economy, has left witness of himself in every man, and that man has only to attend to conscience, as that witness, to know what is right for him to do. On the other side, the Bishop shows or seeks to show, that conscience is not to be identified with any lax maxim of life lived "according to nature," since man's nature is dual and man's duty is to live according to his *higher* nature, which is conscience. Nicely adjusted therefore, as between religion and license, conscience is man's guide par excellence. It is a natural short-cut to deity, graciously available also to honest unbelievers, and a more than natural detour from what is natural but bad. "Let any plain honest man," says Butler, "before he engages in any course of action, ask himself, Is this I am going about right or is it wrong? Is it good, or is it evil? I do not in the least doubt, that this question would be answered agreeably to truth and virtue, by almost any fair man in almost any circumstance."

The Bishop's reasoning grows nice as the difficulty narrows to self-interest. It were easy to ensconce conscience in a secure status if all human impulses that show self-preference were plainly marked bad; but this is where the distinction gets so refined that the reasoning must rise to meet it, or fail of a case for conscience through its drooping powers. Butler is one preacher who simply could not damn as downright bad what seems to bulk so large in men: what the philosophers call egoism and the common man self-interest. Man's self, derived from God, must have something to be said for it. What Butler saw to say was that man is within his *moral* rights when he leans easy on his own dear side. It is a hard saying, for it complicates all else that is to be said. If it is right for man to preoccupy himself with his own concerns—i.e., if "duty" and "interest" are compatible—where do the censors of mankind get their unction in condemning human nature outright as selfish? If self-preference is right, then conscience must approve it. If conscience approves it, does conscience not lose caste as arbiter of rightness?

Bishop Butler finds—and who will say upon reflection that he is wrong? —he finds that many men do not know what their self-interest is. Wisdom is required to be moral; and more wisdom is required, if it be possible, to be moral as touching one's self than as touching others. Self-interest is a real and a legitimate motive for action. Of this Butler is certain, as every moralist who accepts men as they are had better be. But self-interest requires the rectification of a "cool hour" in which the future as dim can equalize the glow of the pressing *now*. Given this "cool hour," connecting one with his *future* self, Butler is willing to abide consequences of the choice made by an intelligent man. "He hath the rule of right within: what is wanting is only that he honestly attend to it."

Conscience must, and through Butler does, come to terms with self-interest. In order to do it, however, Butler, we must admit, has to call in the type of Divine aid which in general he as moralist wills to do without. He would like to show that morality can stand on its own fundations, with conscience alone as its witness. What moralist would not? The Bishop's philosophical pride says: "This faculty was placed within to be our proper governor; to direct and regulate all under principles, passions, and motives of action. This is its right and office; thus sacred is its authority." Out of deference to this moral "radar," as it were, Butler testifies immortally for all the ages to echo: "Had it [conscience], strength as it has right; had it power, as it has manifest authority, it would abso-lutely govern the world."

Such indeed is the Bishop's confidence in conscience that he can afford, at least with a waiver, to be generous to man's impulsive nature. "Conscience and self-love," he declares, "if we understand our true happiness, always lead us the same way." But there is a quiver in his voice to mark the waiver in the contract: "Duty and interest are perfectly coincident," he adds, "for the most part in this world," he adds, "but entirely and in every instance if we take in the future, and the whole," he adds. With this philosophical introduction, he settles down to the "adding" business in earnest: "Those who have been so wise in their generation as to regard only their own supposed interest, at the expense and to the injury of others," he adds, "shall at last find that he who has given up all the advantages of the present world," he adds, "rather than violate his conscience and the relations of life," he adds, "has infinitely better provided for himself, and secured his own interest and happiness."

ETHICAL ALLIANCE WITH THEOLOGY

With professional pain we have quoted the latter passage, but out of fairness we had to do it. We wish that Butler had been able to make out, without extraterritorial resort, that conscience was not only a guide but a rewarder as well—or at least was no less guide for being a poor provider. The Bishop sees that conscience cannot be, in order of nature, both a judge and a power. Seeing that, the danger is that one will also see, or fancy that he sees, that conscience cannot be taken as dependable guide to conduct. Let it be said with Christian pride that Butler does not fall from grace, not far at least, as consequence of insight calculated to make weak men cynical. He weakens a little, as will be more evident when we come to Kant in the chapter, "The Right as the Right." But he weakens only because he can afford to relax: his religious faith gives him leeway to admit of conscience the worst without ceasing to believe of it the best. Given faith in the power of God, Butler keeps his confidence in the guidance of conscience.

If he lost his faith, could he sustain the confidence? We make the question personal, but stay not for the historic answer. Our concern is not with Bishop Butler save as counsel. Conscience, not Butler, is defendant. Suffice it to say of this defendant as competent moral guide that its outstanding weakness is such an "inferiority complex" as to drive it too easily into external alliance to bolster courage. Whoever must rely upon allies is no stronger in general than his crucial alliance. If we are minded to look further into this matter, rather than content ourselves in thankfulness for what we have found in conscience (as we have done in considering other guides to the Right), it is because of fear, borne of experience, that in reaction to the disclosed weakness of any alliance, conscience will lose its grip upon itself. "When I saw the prosperity of the wicked," to paraphrase the psalmist, "then, yes then, my feet almost slipped."

There is unquestionably a tendency in the case of conscience, stronger than in that of other claimants, to presume upon a monopoly of moral guidance. And so there is anxiety as to the flanks of its over-advanced and so highly exposed position. The sense of the "divine" is, as we have seen, autonomous. This sense neither greatly gains nor pathetically loses from the alliance that conscience, as through Butler, claims with it. But conscience tends to claim more than it gains while the alliance prospers, and tends to suffer more in reputation than in character when, for any reason, the alliance is dissolved. Some men, that is, are minded to pitch over everything when their religions undergo a sea-change. Significant as religion is in its own right, even as moral guide, it offers for conscience an equivocal ally.

The alliance tempts conscience to grow presumptuous when it is strong, and leaves it to flounder in isolation when it becomes critical and lonely. On the side of presumption, recall the haughtiness of John Cotton's reply to Roger Williams' charge of persecution for conscience' sake. "We did not drive Williams out of Massachusetts because he followed his conscience," Cotton said substantially; "but because he refused to follow his conscience in doing what he well knew to be right." This is a veritable paradigm in the logic of presumption! And as touching the loneliness of isolation, when the alliance falters, attend in a moment to the classic example of Job.

Men can change, can afford to change, and actually do change religiously in following the gleam of the "divine"—from one sect to another, from one creed to another, and even from the religion of theism to the religion of a-theism—but men cannot afford such radical oscillation in their conscientiousness. They may and should grow at the fringes of conscience, but they cannot afford to play fast and loose with the focus of their own integration. The changes which conscience can afford, and does often need, are themselves made difficult by the dogmas that cluster around institutions devoted to the "divine," and sometimes these necessary changes are rendered dangerous by the power-constellation of the over-organized sacerdotal. Jesus had to drive the bargainers out of the Temple before he could feel free to worship there as in the Temple of God.

It is my earnest desire to protect conscience from any evil effects of its not unnatural alliance with dogma-changers in holy temples and, by way of compensation for any loneliness resulting from its critical independence, to remind conscience that it is never alone, that it has allies also among its own earthly kith and kin. Without losing its sensitivity to the "divine," let it look functionally to the Mannerly, to the Legal, not again to point it to the King of the Tribe, the Categorical. These will offer company without claiming complete custody. These will strengthen its strengths without further weakening its weaknesses.

LOOK TO JOB WHO DOUBTED CONSCIENCE
TO HIS DETRIMENT

For Hebraic-Christian perspective upon this matter, consider Job, Patient Job, and his pious friends: Eliphaz, the Temanite, Bildad, the Shuhite, and Elihu, the Naamathite. Such "friends" they were! Finding Job impoverished, when he had been rich; solitary, when he had been gregarious; diseased when he could even boast that he never had a day's sickness in his whole life; and disturbed, at last, in his faith by the mysterious cumulation of dire events—finding him so, they taxed him thus, taxed him thus for the good of his soul: that since deity rewarded a good conscience with prosperity, adversity argued the presence of something evil within. Job replied that he had done no wrong and that his conscience was clear. Unable to shake him from his sense of conscious integrity, his lovely "friends" turned psychoanalysts and probed for something salacious in his "subconscious." Job swore that he had no secret sins, and dared to declare that if face to face with deity, he could convince Jehovah himself. But when they pounced again and again upon his woes as visible evidence of some necessary, even if unconscious, failing, Job himself was shaken in his moral faith; for he shared with his "friends"—with millions of such friends in every age, including this one!—through a devious and hard theology, the notion that nothing is "Right" save what *Succeeds*. The test of rightness is, therefore, success, if not as the succulence of things paraded, then as "the substance of things hoped for."

This is the test of conscience to which Bishop Butler appealed, though this does not exhaust the doctrine of conscience which he preached. This is the standard harm which religious alliance is likely to do to conscience: it throws conscience completely off-base. This alliance begins with integrity and ends with the final indignity: Might makes Right, to some people otherwise just and sensitive, *if only the scene be laid in Heaven*. It is to them a paralyzing perspective.

ONLY HE IS REALLY GOOD WHO GETS THE GOODS

How pathetically off-base conscience can be thrown may be seen by returning now to the drama of Job, for the last act. This act may have been added by a later hand from some ancient "Hollywood" playwright, a hand with a touch that was sentimental, or punch-drunk on success, or merely cynical; but this *is* the ending, as the drama now stands. Job is humiliated by a voice from the storm, purporting to be Jehovah speaking.

He is so humiliated that he not only eats his words but swallows his conscience as well. The Voice challenges Job with manifestations of *power;*
and demands, as we say, that Job either "put up or shut up." Could Job
match a thunderbolt, hurled like that? "No!" Then let him hold his peace
about Right. Could Job create a hippopotamus—look at those legs "like
tubes of bronze!"—could Job? "No!" Then shut up! Before this brag-
gadacio display of power no less vulgar for being on High, Job surrenders
his soul—What can a man get in exchange for his soul?—surrenders it to
the tune of returning success. He recants in these morally sickening lines:

> I know that thou canst do all things,
> And no plan is too difficult for thee.
> Therefore I have declared, without understanding,
> Things too wonderful for me without knowing.
>
> (42:2-3).

Or does Job really recant? The words are there, and thus they read.
But does one not hear—as conscience hopes?—an undertone that mocks a
tyrant so intent upon display and deference that he takes idle words for
thoughts that are absent, for thoughts that, if present, would be utterly
otherwise? Was Job lying to save his integrity, or indulging in dramatic
tactics to gain time? Or is it all a comedy of manners, immoral but in
tone, to evade the censor, amuse the audience, and vindicate the majesty
of conscience to the discerning?

CONSCIENCE A MIGHTY MORAL MENTOR

Our concern is not really with Job, however, nor yet with exercises in
literary criticism to clear the dramatic record. It is with conscience as
guide to right conduct. It is only that leading which we would illustrate;
only that guidance which we would defend. When properly explained and
adequately defended, what an ever-present guide conscience is in its own
amour-propre!

Conscience, this "friend within," has journeyed with man since man's
journeying began. It reminded Abraham, at the very altar of savage
sacrifice, that the "divine" is not exhausted by the command of gods that
are mean. It grew with man's growth leading that growth as by a light
shining from within. It informed the mannerly with noblesse oblige, and
through mutuality raised good taste from a class-conscious pride into
democratic justice. It has shamed law from its lethargy and prodded it
into a readier response to public opinion so that its own guidance might
leave fewer individual casualties from the march of Right *en masse.*

Conscience has been fortunate in its earthly allies, but its finest fortune has been that it gave more than it got. Those allies which insist that it take more than it gives are not meet allies for conscience; for with them it cannot carry out its dynamic genius.

This genius has flowered more brightly within than without. Its chief radiance is integrated personality. With the multifarious impulses inherited from his animal kin, man stands ever in danger of falling victim to his own variety. If he jumps on the horse of all his desires and rides off in all directions, he goes nowhere—save to the psychiatric clinic. It is conscience that is the principle of integration in man. Its voice it is that keeps him advancing evenly, along all fronts at once. It would be even more accurate, and hardly less honorable, to say that it is to the spirit of integration that we give the name conscience. While the individual advances the front in connecting with other outposts of Rightness—manners, law—he must continually "bring up his own rear." As conscience is the agency of this summation, it becomes also the symbol of the entire advance.

This is in fact the reason for the observation with which we opened this chapter, from Henry Sidgwick, that it can never be an individual's duty to go against his conscience. Though attacking conscience, tough old Thomas Hobbes had declared long before Sidgwick, but in the same spirit, that "it was and ever will be reputed a very evil act for any man to speak against his Conscience." No intelligent person credits conscience with infallibility. It is indeed most fallible, but yet it is sacrosanct. There's the paradox. We have but to observe in order to admit that there are narrow consciences, even fanatical consciences; there are eccentric consciences, infantile consciences, adolescent consciences, arrested consciences; yea, there are even *perverted* promptings, like Adolf Hitler's—

> That fierce thing
> They call a conscience.

Yet, conscience must never be violated, however fierce or foolish. A paradox, indeed! Follow your conscience, all persons, everywhere, and always, as Ruskin advises; but first make certain—and here Ruskin partly expunges the paradox—make certain that "it is not the conscience of an ass!"

There always remains something of the atmosphere of a paradox, hanging over the true and just prescription: *Don't desert your conscience!* The wisdom of the injunction is that you must always be *bringing up your reserves,* if your advance is to hold its ground. You must, that is, be one person, not many. It is conscience that keeps you one, and it alone can keep you unified enough to make you effective as a person. He who reaps from an outraged conscience a sense of guilt, an inexpungeable stain of shame, will always, like Lady Macbeth, be daubing at his splotches—

> Out, damned spot!—out, I say!

rather than attending wholeheartedly to the business in hand. Through chronic disconcertion, he becomes a person good for nothing, because he is not really and fully one person at all. He is not all there, does not carry himself with him. He is, in short, a *divided* self, fluttering in the division, spilling his energies in the interstices of what should have been a single selfhood.

The final case for conscience, then, as guide to Right, is negative. At the least, it tells us, as it told Socrates, what not to do. At the very least it tells us not to desert ourselves. Its positive function we have also explored. Its advantages we have cited. Its allies we have appraised. Its contributions we have estimated. But if in the darkness of some night one wishes to counter the worst that temptation can offer with the strongest that can be said for this monitor, this is the final word: conscience can never be disobeyed with impunity. Nobody can ever prove it utterly wrong; for even when it is mistaken, it is still not right to violate conscience. No, it can never be wholly wrong to obey conscience; it can never be fully right to disobey it. With this negative assurance, conscience may raise its head, proudly above all inferiority feelings, to carry on its indispensable work. There will always be a conscience.

In this utter security, its bounden duty becomes to keep itself informed so that we, who are its glad wards, may—

> . . . grow from more to more,
> As more of reverence in us dwells,
> That mind and heart according well,
> May make one music as before,
>
> But vaster.

If you would find and do the Right, keep your conscience, then, on the grow, decipher it, obey it. As minimum reward for such devotion, we are prepared to guarantee that when you call upon yourself, you will always find yourself at home. It is more than can be said for many modern men.

The Right is verily the Conscientious, the conscientious and more.

CHAPTER 5

THE RIGHT AS THE RIGHT

As aspiring pilgrims toward the Right, we have long been climbing —climbing, however, what some ethicists would regard as but the foothills of morality: skirting manners, laws, consciences for insight into right living. Mere foothills, if indeed more than molehills, the more austere would say. We have ourselves looked with prouder eyes than they upon the vistas yielded by these several vantages; but this is because we have had to regard with a more weather-beaten eye the human scene. Only those can spurn such vistas who have a point of view transcendingly superior. We come from what we have regarded as respectable eminences now to scale what has been regarded as the very Matterhorn of morality— the categorical as monopolistic claimant of the heights of Rightness.

Lesser names are carved on the approaches to this Great Stone Face of ethical aspiration, but that of Immanuel Kant stands glowing down upon all the rest. Here is a spiritual hero who, seeing the problematic to which the Christian tradition often got sunk, set out to rise above all swamps and bogs, all hills and crevices, to claim at last the dizzying heights of purest rationality in the name of ethics. His pride was to overtop the Problematic by gaining a crag from which the view would be both *compelling* and *limitless.*

This ambitious pilgrim, Immanuel Kant, was a German of the 18th century who took seriously the challenge to philosophy made by scientific advances. Himself not untrained in science, Kant sought to bring a Copernican revolution to philosophy. Man could not know what was impossible for him to know, nor do what lay quite beyond human powers. In general, Kant asked himself how man, with finite capacities, could know things infinite in scope and reach. And the answer was, in general, that man could not know the infinite. He could know only what his capacities

fitted him to know. There may be a realm of reality beyond the scientific
—Kant thought so—but such a realm can not be known to be. He proved,
or thought he proved, the impossibility of disproving such knowledge;
and so he left through the impossibility of disproof room for belief in
what is admittedly beyond the reach of knowledge.

So much in general. In particular, Kant served ethics (and religion)
as defense and then as release. He found in man himself more than man
the animal could explain. This "more" it is now our business to disclose
and our privilege to celebrate.

THE GOOD WILL AS FINAL GOOD

But we ourselves shall do well to approach this towering "more"
through humble steps which we can retrace if the going gets too tough.
Life early teaches us that some "goods" are good *for* other goods. We
count wealth good, but good because of benefits other than itself, which
it brings in its train. Otherwise it is the disease of miserliness. Wealth is
good: it is good for health, it is good for comfort, it is good for adventure,
it is good for power—and what else not?

But what are these good for? Some are good for some ends and others
for others. But is there not something that is good without the deprecia-
tion "good for"? Is there not something that is simply good, good in
itself, good without regard to consequence (*intrinsically good*)? Now,
it may be that each intermediate step is in some small part good in itself,
while mostly being valued as a means to something else. But are there
not some things, at least one thing, we insist, that is sheerly and simply
good—an end which is end to all means and itself means to none? If so,
that would indeed be the *summum bonum:* ethical fulfilment at last, at
long last for the pilgrim's eager soul.

Immanuel Kant found what he thought to answer to this precious
finality. It is not, not to begin with, anything that man wills; it is, rather,
man's aspiration itself. In short and in full, we find our answer in the
"Good Will." But is that not too simple?—And, besides, it is circular.
Let us survey the matter further on this easy grade of Goodness before
we approach the crags of Rightness, to which Kant's enterprise is pointed.

The Will of which Kant speaks is not a faculty that finds its fulfilment
in the fruits of action, and certainly not in the meadows of pleasurable
feelings. It is worlds away from any rewards of the pig sty, this disposi-
tion in which men find a good "not because the consequences which flow
from it are good, nor because it is capable of attaining the end which it

seeks, but . . . is good in itself or because it wills the good . . . and its intrinsic value is in no way increased by success or lessened by failure." Not only does such a treasure, as the good will is thus described, tower above all lesser values, but it gives to them their meaning, and from it they borrow their dignity. "No doubt," as Kant goes on to admit, "it is . . . a desirable thing to have intelligence, sagacity, judgment, and other intellectual gifts . . . ; it is also good and desirable in many respects to possess by nature such qualities as courage, resolution, and perseverance; but all these . . . may be in the highest degree pernicious and hurtful, if the will which directs them . . . is not itself good."

The grand conclusion to which this connoisseur of the categorical arrives is this: "Nothing in the whole world, or even outside of the world, can possibly be regarded as good without limitation except a *good will*." And for those whose attention wanders from the echoes of these arid heights to the greener valleys below, Kant adds: "A good will would therefore seem to be the indispensable condition without which no one is even worthy to be happy."

FOLLOWING THE CLUES

Little doubt that such insight and such eloquence ring some bell in every man's soul: in some a bell of warning of emptiness if not of austerity; in others the bell of spiritual fulfilment. One phrase of Kant's may well prompt every student to look farther: a good will is one which, in a single phrase (above), "wills the good." The genius of Kant was in following the leading of the "good will" until he achieved the Right, to which it pointed. If willing is a mere *form* of striving which requires a content to complete it (and this is the commonest view of "will"), then what is it that the "good will" *wills* to make it fully "good," good in substance as well as in form? Kant, more than most philosophers, has warned us against concepts "empty" of perceptual content. It is indeed in seeking content against his skepticism that Kant comes to his ultimate doctrine of the Right.

The *content* of the willing that is good is found to be not an object as of a desire, but a law; or if an object, then law as the object. If it were the will of an animal, the object willed might be a pleasure or other type of sensuous delight. This might indeed be true of man's will, since man is an animal too; might be that, but may be more than that—and the "more" become a *must* when man stretches to his full human height. Man, though animal, is at the same time rational; and so, since capable of judgment, is obligated to judge. What man of "necessity" judges, and judges to be "universal," becomes to his will, as itself on one side rational, the final good, that indeed which makes the "good will" *good*.

The law, therefore, which the good will accepts as its rational vocation is the content which reason furnishes the will. Man, thus, legislates to himself: his reason giving orders which the will as animal resists but which the will as rational accepts. Of such inward striving is obligation born. It is to no point at all that the will does not always obey, but it is everything that it acknowledges obligation. It is man's glory to find a law, this obligation, in his own household, whatever he does about it. "Conscious of its own dignity," as Kant says, "the moral law treats all sensuous desires with contempt, and is able to master them one by one." By "master" Kant does not mean that the obligation always gets obeyed, but that at least it gets deferred to as what the will when rational accepts to be its limit if not its goal.

"HYPOTHETICAL IMPERATIVES"

The content of the willing that is good is, let us repeat, a law: a self-legislated obligation, if you will. But as there are goods and goods, so there are laws and laws. Duty has at least a speaking acquaintance with prudence; and "right" gets confused as between calculation and conscience. We say, in easygoing fashion, that it is right to follow the doctor's orders, but that is because we want to get well; that we ought to pay our debts, but that is because we want present repute and future credit; that we ought to listen to our banker or broker, but that is because we want to prosper. We "ought" to do, that is, *what we have to do if we are to get what we want.* That is, of course, an everyday meaning of Right, a homely exemplification of Duty. But it is not a "disinterested" meaning of either. It is not what they look like from the highest eminence. It is, on the negative side, but to illustrate what Thomas Hobbes, the 16th Century English philosopher, put so pithily and even wittily against the critics of his *Leviathan*—Thomas Hobbes, that *diabolus* of all Kantian apostles of "disinterestedness": "That I made the civil power too large, *but this by ecclesiastical persons;* that I had utterly taken away liberty of conscience, *but this by sectaries;* that I had set the princes above the laws, *but this by lawyers.*" (Italics mine.)

"THE CATEGORICAL IMPERATIVE"

Each man, this is, to his own hog-wash, calling it of course by a name more conscience-salving than swill. All this is but to spell out, how-

ever, what Thomas Carlyle—a British Kantian—called "pig-trough" philosophy. And it is to bring us back to an ambiguity in the Right which
we have already illustrated in the Good. The self-legislated law—Kant's
final Right—in which the will finds its Good is not something right as
a means, upon the hypothesis that some desired end depends upon it. Far
from it. It is a law which states what one's duty is for *every possible
occasion:* and that means, too, for *every possible man.* There are to it no
"ifs" and "ands." It is "universal" and it is "necessary."

Bring forth your occasion, entertain the promptings to action which the
occasion suggests to your will, and then test these empirical promptings
by a law non-empirical, the law that has arisen out of your own nature
simply because it is a rational nature that you have. That law, which tests
all actions for rightness and is in its goodness tested by none, is this, as
Kant first formulates it: "In all cases I must act in such a way *that I can
at the same time will that my maxim should become a universal law.*"

That is a law which is *the* law indeed: the Categorical Imperative.
In subsequent formulations of this law, Kant seems to depart from will
as fulfilled in law-as-such and to seek an object of desire to furnish content to the willing. But that is a story for another chapter, the story of
Kant's compensation for austerity. We accept here his early rigor as our
categorical meed, and overlook any inconsistency he may have developed.
Our aim is not here to exhaust Kant but to explain the categorical with
which Right sometimes gets identified, best of all in Kant's philosophy.

The obligation which Kant thus lays upon the will as its final object
and ultimate fulfilment would transmute any action informed of it from
a spurt of animal energy into an adventure of the spirit, any temporal
want into a timeless aspiration, and any deed from a commonplace doing
into an achievement lighted by the moral light that never was on land or
sea. Through such an acceptance the will of man escapes its own animal
doom of glutting after "wants" and finds itself in "reverence" for a worthy
object: As Kant feelingly describes it, "reverence for law." Every self-
conscious act becomes through this exercise a moral pageant in which
will not only transcends its animal heats but arrives at the Mecca of radi-
ant morality: pure morality as distinct from the impurities portrayed in
our preceding chapters. No inclination now enters in at all, for if duty
were done for any other reason than reverence for law, it would cease to
be duty. The individual is thus not merely budged from what he was
to what he may be, but by the same token of rationality he arrives at
what man, who was animal, has become as spirit, and indeed arrives
within sight of what man may become as immortal soul. The purview
of such transfigured will is all time and every place; its companionship

is every rational being, and its destiny is a spiritual community in which what is law to one is law to all; for all is for each and each is for all in the "Kingdom of Ends" founded in and bounded by the rationality of such universal and necessary willing.

This Categorical Imperative is the Will of God (Who has made us rational) operating as a principle of grace through the rationality of man upon the world of nature. It is the Conscience of man raised in true Teutonic form to the *n*th degree:

> *Conscience, conscience über alles,*
> *Über alles in der Welt.*

Such is the vision which Immanuel Kant had of man's moral potentiality. It is full of dignity; it leaves man as his own legislator, and appears more than other moral systems as adequate self-provider. It is austere in that it requires man to grow up to the maturity of full belief in functional equality. No more easy exceptions of ego out of the "noble impartiality of self-preference." We have here the most defensible statement of what the Golden Rule apparently intends; full equality of man by nature and utter impartiality in treatment. Rationality is the same in all, and its exercise bears witness to human commonalty.

A LAW NOT DEPENDENT UPON PRACTICE

Kant's is a vision neither sired from nor shamed by practice. He admits that such austere actions as the Categorical Imperative enjoins "perhaps never have been done." This is too bad, not for man's Reason, but for his un-reason. The demand of Reason remains what it is, let the chips of failure fall where they may. The pathos which surrounds Kant's philosophy is born of man's ambivalence, and reflects upon the lower self alone. The part of man's will which is not rational wants many things which it cannot get through duty, and must indeed forego because of duty. Man's "supreme good"—the distinction is Kant's—is acceptance of the demand of rationality as the human vocation; but man's "complete good" would be to get as reward for that acceptance what the acceptance does not entail, cannot guarantee—happiness. Ethics, therefore, as the Law of the Ought, leaves man only half fulfilled, but fulfilled in his nobler half. How Kant seeks, and thinks he finds, the other half of fulfilment, in theology, is itself a thrilling story, but one not to be pursued here.

If the student thinks that Kant's insight is only "vision," let him remember what he has been learning right along: that no theory begets full-bodied practice. No moral maxim implements itself, nor does any provide the vitamin which directly produces the perfect performance. *That* each individual himself alone can provide. Though morality is the theory of practice, it is not at the same time the practice of its theory. All Kant asks is what every moralist asks: your life. He can ask no more; nor will he take less. For living, including right living, is a venture. Life is a gamble, but since we must take it, we had better make the gamble circumspect. In the end, if we cheat, we rob only ourselves.

THE PRECIOUS LOOK BEFORE THE LEAP

Since life is a leap, the look is the least we can provide for the hazard. It is the magnificence of Kant's "look" that makes him so great a friend to every aspiring soul. His system, he thinks, is morality *as such;* all else is irrelevant. Though Kant's high *a priorism* does not thrill us as much as it did Kant, we would be lacking candor, which we have everywhere sought to exemplify constructively, if we did not say, here at the end as we have intimated throughout, how breathless is Kant's vision, how inspiring his prescription. Any man who can meet face to face, understandingly, "the moral law within" without obeisance could indeed look out into stellar space on a brilliant night, as neither Kant nor we can do, without a curtsy to the gallant cosmos: both material macrocosm and moral microcosm.

Kant's undertaking is thrilling for its very austerity. Better to fail in such summit stalking than to succeed lolling safely on the ground. And yet it is not appropriate, not really, to speak of "failure" in connection with Kant. Man's only failure here would be to fall short of understanding his high estate as a rational animal. Understanding is the one achievement that is self-rewarding. The primary question is not one of living up to what the Categorical Imperative demands. As we have seen, Kant has no perfectionistic expectations as touching practice. He knows how complex human nature is, and what its undertows from the rational. He is concerned about practice—as what honest man with good glands is not?—but his particular task is to find whether in human nature itself there is *basis,* a rational foundation, for civilized practice. If Kant has found that, who is to say, in our necessitated division of intellectual labor, that Kant has not done his part? It is enough, or at least nearly enough, for us to see that he has actually done that.

The best proof in ethics, though not necessarily satisfying to a logical positivist, is to ask for honest judgment from the reader. Have you understood what Kant is driving at? Do you find something in yourself that answers to his demand that, if you want to honor your "rational"

nature, you must necessarily universalize your judgments? Do you thrill
to his exaction that you must count yourself as one, as but one, as an
equal member of a community of rational beings where all are treated as
ends in themselves, not as mere means to the ends of others? If you can
answer these questions in the affirmative, Kant has won his war with you.
The intensity of your "applause meter" will measure the extent to which
you are now a Kantian. You could do much worse than to be a full and
proud Kantian; for to be really so but means to understand as well as to
honor the Golden Rule.

And yet who ever saw anybody, up to the hilt, *practicing* the Golden
Rule? The Golden Rule, you remember—or do you?—was given to the
world in the context of advice that if somebody, anybody, slaps your one
cheek, you turn the other cheek; that if a robber takes your coat, you give
him your overcoat, etc. When have you seen any American *practicing*
that?

On any moral theory, practice has to take care of itself the best it can.
And that "best" is always *better* when it is adorned with good manners.
This knowledge has already informed our earlier chapters, and is now
at your disposal for whatever compensations you may feel beyond the
call of Kant. But Kant is far from having no relevance for practice, if you
begin by allowing him the leeway which you must allow yourself, whatever your theory.

Kant's prescription is helpful because it sustains generality, without
which no practice can be wise. His vision of pure rationality, *necessary*
and *universal,* gives perspective, whatever it does not give; it yields catharsis, whatever it does not yield; it fortifies human dignity, whatever it
fails to fulfill. To discover that animal conscience, indigenous but crass,
can be refined from fanaticism and cruelty into judgment that surmounts
self-preference and bids for equality among men, this is to give confidence
to the old and noble faith of the American Fathers in "the perfectibility
of mankind"; this is indeed to span the gulf between animal felicity and
rational blessedness.

The test of this is to find whether other moralists, whatever their general view, must sustain something like Kant's demands before they can
make their moral theory respectable. David Hume, who taught Kant
much on the side of skepticism, confirms Kant's wisdom on the side of
moral practice. Hume, who scouted the "rational" in Kant's sense and
who outraged Kant's austerity by declaring that "reason is and ought
to be the slave of the passions," this Hume has, nevertheless, described
the function of reason as that of "scouting out the land" so that, as between the "passions," we may give rein to the better and wiser emotion.

Perspective is imperative to save any moral system from debasement, and this is the essence of what Kant achieves on the side of practice.

No moralist dare do less, therefore, than his best to grasp Kant's vision, though he may thereafter think to combine with reverence for law the fruits of earth and time—on earth, in time. In doing so, he will be well advised, however, to reverence Kant negatively—*not to do what he cannot honestly universalize.* This is surely *one* pathway, indeed a highroad, to the Right. On the leeward side of this categorical imperative, man may still pay his money and take his chance. But let him look before he leaps, and then leap to live as well as possible.

The Moral is indeed the Right, the Right and more: it is also the Good.

BOOK II

THE ETHICAL AS THE GOOD

We have finished the first part of our investigation of the moral: How to find and to do the Right. Without exhausting the notion of rightness, we have seen its affiliates and have profited from its spread. We come now to do the same service to ethics from another, the other, point of view: the Good. Seen from within, our conduct seems always fulfilling or thwarting desire. We assume as goal of desire the Good; and this as operative in the world is the norm of our conduct. As for the Right, others ought to do it—and we too, incidentally. We are ourselves privileged to realize the Good—and others too, incidentally. What is common between these different points of view is the bridge on which we now pass to Book II: How to discover and to possess the Good.

It is not likely, however, that Good is simply and merely something else. Good is good, and that's that; save only that that is not enough. Satisfaction of our desires is so important to us that we cannot rest with a mere intuition of an identity. We need to increase its quality, to circumvent its opposition, evil; and to regulate our conduct with reference to its efficiency for and against what we desire. So we are now to study its context, as we have studied the context of the Right. Nothing with which we have sought to identify the Right has exhausted it. But we are the wiser for the attempt, and we shall be the wiser here, for exploring the ecology of the Good.

Different men at different times and under different circumstances have said that Good is this or that or the other. If any be right in what they have said, it is important to us; if all be wrong, or only partially right, it need not, even so, prove unimportant to us. Our own modesty, born of ignorance, leads us to learn from all, assuming value in each. The more we see, therefore, with what Good has been and is now being associated, the better we can identify it in the complex of life; and the more chance, it would appear, we have to maximize it, whatever it may prove to be in itself.

For this reason, and in this faith, we turn now to the clues furnished us by our own reflection, and by willing witnesses, living and dead.

CHAPTER 6

THE GOOD AS THE PLEASURABLE

Changing gears now from the backward look, or the inward, or the upward—that is, from the source out of which proceed acts that are moral—we take the forward look. From the Right indeed, we turn now to the Good. The simplest—at least the most simple-seeming—end to which men have looked for a good that justifies effort and climaxes life, is *pleasure*. Action is purposive, at least the action peculiar to man is purposive. Pleasure is an ancient, and let us say at once an honorable, way of tying purpose to an end. There is little if anything that even other theories hold good which is not deferred to in the hedonistic purview.

INTRINSIC VS. EXTRINSIC GOOD

"You want wealth?"

"Yes, I want wealth. With Hilaire Belloc,

> I'm tired of Love; I'm still more tired of Rhyme;
> But Money gives me pleasure all the time."

"You cannot eat it, you know!"

"No, not literally. But I can buy things to eat, to wear, comfort to live in, hospitality for friends, discomfiture to enemies: in fact all the things that are enjoyable seem to stay for wealth."

"Then it is pleasure that justifies your wealth-seeking!"

"You want fame! What for? It is ephemeral, you know."

"Yes, I know; but it is so good while it lasts: to be well thought of, to be deferred to, to be enhanced inwardly by the buoyancy of outer esteem."

"You seem to me to be saying that you *enjoy* it."

"Yes, I do enjoy fame, what little I have tasted; and I would willingly have any amount more."

"It is pleasure, then, that justifies your pursuit of what you call fame."

"Yes, it is pleasure as an end which informs with meaning fame as a means. As Milton sang:

> Fame is the spur that the clear spirit doth raise
> To scorn delights, and live laborious days."

"You want God. What for?"

"Well, in the language of the creed, and in the spirit of the faithful, 'to enjoy Him forever'!"

"You want immortality. What for?"

"So that I may enjoy indefinitely a life which in this mundane stretch I have found pleasurable."

"You want to do good; don't answer why, for I now know the answer without being told: you *enjoy* doing good."

"Estimating now your spiritual profile from all that has gone before, I can see how happy you are when you are hospitable."

"You seem to imply that I am thinking of myself in whatever I do for other people."

"No, you are thinking of them. You are the kind of person who does think of others, the kind of person who gets pleasure from giving pleasure. You do not need to think of yourself in order to get pleasure from wealth, or fame, or from doing good. But if you rippled on the shallows sometimes and had to look for a reason, that reason would be that you get pleasure from your way of life. I know this because I know that you wouldn't likely make money, get fame, or do good if you were so built that any such activity gave you pain. Pleasure is the end to which appeal can always be made if an end be required to justify activity."

HEDONISM IN REVERSE

More important, if possible, is it, at times, to censure the actions of others. As we have seen, the ethics of Right gets a head start upon any ethics of the Good. We are dependent as infants before we can begin to show independence as youths. While we are learning what is "good" experimentally, we are having to act by rules of what is "right," as defined for us by others, and sometimes defined contrary to our personal views. The inherited rules of society sometimes indeed bear very hard upon men. Especially is this true in a society aristocratic enough to make what brings pain to humble men the rule of reason for others to whom it brings pleasure.

AN ILLUSTRATION FROM ITALY

A young Italian nobleman told me during the war in Italy that he would shoot the first peasant who asked him, communist-wise, for a piece of the nobleman's ancestral land. "And," added he defensively, "you will not say that my act would not be reasonable."

"No," I admitted as I invited him to our mess for further talk, "I would not say your act was not reasonable." "To be reasonable," I continued at dinner, "means two different things in English. It means, first, to fulfill expectations. In this sense your act would be reasonable: you expect this reaction of yourself; your friends expect it of you; and I dare say from long experience with your kind the peasant expects it of you." But I added: "Reasonable as it is, it is a most unfortunate act which you project. There are many peasants and few sons of the aristocracy. When the shooting is over, there will still be many peasants left, and no sons of the aristocracy."

He admitted that that was precisely what was worrying him.

"Then," continued I, "you are not wholly unprepared for the other meaning of the term 'reasonable.' It is also reasonable," I continued, "to do the act that would produce on the whole the most desirable consequences. Since you hardly desire to be killed and only circumspectly desire to kill, it *is* unreasonable for you to start with the peasant a process that will end in many getting killed, including you."

"What is the average holding of land in Italy?" I inquired. He replied that it was only a few acres of land.

"Would his peasants be satisfied with this average?" I questioned.

He replied that they would, would be surprised and gratified.

"And would this leave you land?" I persisted.

He admitted that it would leave him with thousands of acres.

"Then," concluded I, "since you identify your pleasure (and duty) with their continued deprivation, do I apprehend that you propose to do yourself to the death by performing your aristocratic duty?"

He admitted that it was so—and went away not only sad but offended.

Pain is more easily identified than is many another criterion of evil. Not even the humblest man can be shown to be wholly mistaken when he thinks that he suffers pain. His thinking so, up to a point, makes it so. To have the reliance of a standard which nobody can beat anybody out of, this is a strong point in any theory of ethics. Here it redounds to the honor and utility of hedonism.

HEDONISM DEFINED

Combining the availability of pleasure to locate the Good and the practicality of using pain to identify the bad, we may now define our present philosophy as holding that *pleasure and only pleasure is good, that pain and only pain is bad*. This is the philosophy from of old called hedonism (from the Greek word meaning pleasure). Of course, in such a definition reference is to *intrinsic* value: the quality of being good in itself, rather than merely producing desirable consequences. Our primary concern, here and later, is with good as an end.

The ease of identity which pleasure offers and the equality of appeal furnished by its immanence make hedonism a recurring doctrine in the moral history of mankind. The presence and use of pleasure constitute hedonism a good pleader for life itself as a self-justifying enterprise. "I came into this world," said Thoreau in high cogency, "not chiefly to make this a good place to live in, but to live in it. . . ." Through such emphases is hedonism justified positively, as it is justified negatively by the zeal with which reformers of differential privilege turn to it in the clinches of history. If the Italian peasant appealed to justice, he would at once be disqualified by Italian law—made by the aristocrats. If he appealed to God, he would be at once taught his duty by the Church, which as an agency of order stands for obedience to constituted authority. If he appealed to natural law, second nature would shame him into silence. When he points simply to his pains, he can, but can hardly, be beaten out of his convictions regarding his deserts.

Utilitarianism is as good a theoretical example of the negative potency of hedonism as we require. Not only did Jeremy Bentham declare that pleasure is the only good, pain the only bad; but he levelled all intra-hedonic pretenses by declaring also that "pushpin is as good as poetry," provided it have in it as much pleasure. Such "quantitative" hedonism need not be emphasized, for it is, strictly speaking, the only kind there is. Hedonism should either mean what it says, or learn to say what it means. What it means is, as we have observed, the simple doctrine that pleasure and pain are identical with good and bad, with no over-lapping of either. Of course the more pleasure, then, the more good; the more pain, the more evil.

SIDE-ISSUES ONLY CHARILY SIDE-STEPPED

Let us now complicate this clarity of the obvious by issues adventitious to strict logic but relevant to an ethics of conduct. Such side-issues are: whether we all always seek pleasure and only pleasure (Psychological Hedonism); whether pleasure and only pleasure is what we ought to seek (Ethical Hedonism); whether to get pleasure, it is better to forget it altogether (Hedonistic Paradox); whether pleasure is better found in intellectual than in physical activities (Rationalistic Hedonism); whether in contemplation than in problem-solving (Aesthetic Hedonism); and whether one man's pleasure is as important as another man's (Democratic Hedonism). However these issues stand logically, they are close concerns of any theory of practice. We shall discuss them in this text, in and out of this chapter, wherever they appear to be most fruitful. We shall do this without displacing from the fore what is foremost in hedonism: that in pleasure and pain we have not only intelligible but defensible goals for the good life.

What we have just called "Democratic Hedonism" may now be remarked at once, because it bears fruitfully upon the negative utility of hedonism, which we have already introduced. It should appear plain to the point of obviousness that if pleasure be good, as the theory keeps to the fore, then one man's is as good as another's. Abstractly this is so, and would hardly be concretely questioned if men did not so clearly differ one from another. Since at any given time, in almost every observable regard, men do differ, may not one man's pleasure be better than another's even on strict logical grounds? The denial of this by Bentham— "each to count for one and nobody for more than one"—has constituted Benthamite hedonism a reform movement as well as an ethical doctrine. By asserting something to be true—namely, that pleasure is pleasure wherever found—it was actually tearing down social distinctions justified only if one man was better than another. The way in which this so-called "Founder of the Modern World" came to formulate egalitarianism as a part of the ethics of hedonism is instructive.

HOW ETHICS BECOMES SOCIAL THEORY AND
POLITICAL ACTION

Bentham himself belonged to a class above the medium in England, a class which once at least assumed that unequal distribution of wealth was justified by different capacities of men for goodness. It was natural that he should regard the greatest happiness principle as obvious; it *was* obvious, but obviously a justification of class distinctions. So he at first put it the Greatest Happiness not of all but of the Greatest Number. Soon he saw that this too was a class investment. Since some men are more sensitive than others, and so more deserving, the way to get the greatest happiness out to everybody is to emphasize the superior rights of Somebodies.

Bentham tells his own story of the discovery of this inter-incidence of moral theory and social distinctions, and it is a story which made him turn to political action to resolve what he thought a poor articulation of the other two. He once believed, he said, that it would be enough to call the attention of the upper strata, his friends that is, to the greatest happiness principle in order to get them to do justice in the alleviation of pains and in the equalization of access to the means of pleasure. It proved not enough, for the simple reason that his friends actually thought greater general happiness resulted by giving superior opportunities to superior people. So as a political sledge-hammer he added the final and radical qualification to the Greatest Happiness of the Greatest Number, "each to count for one and nobody for more than one."

Now all this is, in strict logic, only collateral to hedonism, as our first teleological theory of ethics. But it has something to do, nevertheless, has in fact much to do with hedonism as a theory of the good life. Ethics is not logic after all. The Good cannot be tied up neatly and kept sterile, not the good-for-man, the concrete and striving animal. Since the human is not some Platonic Man, but is men, there is no moral theory that does not get dented in the human struggle for advantage. This had best be recognized, since it is so; and a moral theory of Goodness carries some obligation, therefore, of oughtness against being prostituted to ends nonmoral, and certainly against ends that are immoral.

Hedonism has often been thought of by its enemies as contributing to the degradation of human character. We are ourselves prepared, however, as in connection with each theory gone before or theory to come after, prepared to find in hedonism whatever good it actually has—and we assume that what has lived for centuries and what recurs again and again at human crises does contain much good. Before passing, therefore, to its defense against the charge of its being immoral, let us balance its accounts:

AN ASSESSMENT OF HEDONISM

1. As a pure statement of positive fact, that *pleasure is always good, pain always bad,* we have no doubt that hedonism is true and important. Spinoza, for all his rigor, affirms both these convictions.

2. As an exclusive doctrine, that *only pleasure is good, only pain is bad,* hedonism is probably false, neatly taken. It has its defenses, however; and may prove useful even in error.

3. As a social doctrine, of the equality of men, hedonism is as sound as Christianity, as sound and more concrete.

4. As a political doctrine of reform, hedonism is highly useful. It is indeed a singularly effective means to prevent some men from being continually beaten out of their argument for a chance to become more than they are, or even to maintain themselves for what they are.

In general we may say that hedonism is right in what it affirms, wrong in what it denies. On the positive side, it makes a quick case for itself. Nor is its case less permanent than quick, for men are always getting obfuscated and diverted, not only from justice to others but also from the most immediate self-goods, by their moral theories, which run all too easily to fanaticism of faith and from that to denial of the will to live. Hedonism is, as we have seen, a simple reliance against wrongs too grossly inflicted in the name of some intrenched Right. Whether good *means* pleasure and only pleasure, as the rigorous hedonist insists, it needs little proof that pleasure *is* good, and surely no proof at all that pain is *bad.*

HEDONISTIC DEFENSES AGAINST MISUSE

This theory of the Good, which seems the least in need of positive proof, can be turned on the negative side very quickly into something not wholly irreproachable. Somehow or other, hedonism is always on the defensive. Pleasures get into such trouble, I mean, with pleasures that thought cannot rest from their troubling—and cannot do much about their quarrels save to change the venue. So long as pleasures don't quarrel, so to say, hedonism is the easiest and may well be the best of moral philosophies. At any rate we must be prepared to appropriate every ounce of benefit it affords. But simple appropriation does not reach far or last long. Pleasure seems to have a genius for trouble, not merely quarrelling with Duty, as moralists of the Right always complain, but doubling back to quarrel with itself, as moralists of the Good must observe and deplore.

This comes about so chronically that it is complained historically, and not without some reason, that hedonism leads easily to cynicism. The Cyrenaic of youth becomes the cynic of middle-age, and then matures as the grouch of dotage. (It may be better, even so, to be a grouch with present memories than a saint with a hidden past!) Since, however, every moral philosophy has its problems, about which we can do little, we ought to lend a hand to each from all, when the termites of doubt begin their silent work. They will be at our own foundations when they have finished with our neighbor's. There is not indeed more wisdom than we need in *all* the moral theories. If hedonism has its problems, it has its defenses too.

PSYCHOLOGICAL HEDONISM

The first reinforcement it has against the discouragement that the pleasure-principle meets because of family troubles is to affirm loudly, because defensively, that, nevertheless, men seek pleasure; that indeed it is the only thing that men do consciously seek as the Good. This is what is called Psychological Hedonism: that pleasure is what as a matter of fact men do naturally seek.

Now there can be little doubt that some men at least do sometimes at least seek pleasure; but that all men do all the time seek it alone is more than doubtful. Men seem more naturally to seek money, and power, and fame, and love, on the same level with pleasure. And on a lower logical but humanely a more concrete level, men seem to seek objects, and not objects alone that give pleasure. They seem to seek high mountains to climb, which yield danger and fatigue and pain. They hunt out tasks because they are dutiful and even because the tasks go downright against the grain of pleasureful desires. It can also be pointed out, though I do not think it fair or fruitful to overweight it against a wobbling comrade-theorist, that it is sick men who seek pleasures rather than arduous endeavors; men with jaded appetites hunt pleasure rather than a juicy beefsteak, men with morbid desires keep their minds on pleasure or sex rather than upon woman-adored or man-revered. Healthy appetite wants food, not a psychological derivative; and the healthy lover is one who is so lost to his object that he can say, with a poet, "And now she [he] doesn't remind me of anyone any more."

It is pointed out, indeed, that activities and objects and persons are the natural and the primary objects of the desires of man, the active animal; and that objects of thought, like thought itself, come later upon the evolutionary scene. If this be so—and it appears so—then all psychological affiliates and derivatives must take a subordinate place in moral theory.

To make objects secondary and psychology primary to morality is morbid to begin with and neurotic in the end.

THE HEDONISTIC PARADOX

Hedonism has felt the impact of this line of argument so often that its predicament has been made exemplary; it has been made to bear, that is, the brunt of a paradox common to all theories: to *get* pleasure . . . *forget* it. This paradox, which is real enough, warns the hedonist of a path not less hazardous to him from being dangerous to all. To make even virtue a self-conscious goal is more likely to turn out a prig than a man of robust morality. Thus from the hedonistic predicament we have relearned wisdom for all our theories: not to make the theoretical the goal of theory, but, with Justice Holmes, *"to think things."*

To think, however, even "to think things," requires that we have something to think with: concepts, or in the value field *norms*. The hedonist, driven from a psychology that is inadequate, need not yet acknowledge total defeat. He has lost a skirmish in the foothills, but he yet holds the summit. Certainly he has not lost the war. If he yields the notion that men merely seek pleasure, he may still hold that the standard by which we judge our seeking is pleasure. On the way from Psychological Hedonism [that men do seek pleasure] he may try to hold the pass of Ethical Hedonism [pleasure is at any rate what men *ought* to seek]; but if he is driven from that, he can fall back with more security upon the plain brand of which we have spoken [calling it Authentic Hedonism]: that since all action must be judged by norms, pleasure is the norm by which moral action is finally to be adjudged, whatever it is that men seek or ought to seek. This was the way that John Stuart Mill trod on his pilgrimage from Bentham, whether he thus reached moral Mecca or not.

If Hedonism sheds its totalitarianism of claim and accepts aid (as Mill did) from, as well as gives help to, other theories in trouble with the problematic, it is difficult to see how hedonism can be driven from the field of moral theory. It is one right theory; and it can be shown wrong only by another right theory borrowing the presumption with which hedonism began, that there is only one right theory. And any theory would probably break its own back with the weight of such presumption, leaving the other theories standing erect over its ruins. Admitting pleasure one of the goods of life, the pleasure-principle would seem to be one of the permanent possibilities of rationalizing morality.

This theory has certainly proved useful in the evolution of justice. Any act that produces more pain in the world than is inevitable while effecting its own peculiar good, is a wrong act in any decent man's language. And that may well be allowed to be the *reason* that such an act is wrong. Indeed any act that unnecessarily sacrifices pleasure, whatever of good it otherwise effects, is to that extent a wrong act. To state it fully, any act that produces any pleasure or avoids any pain is to that extent, pro or con, a right act. Since pleasure is a good, we cannot deny it honorable place as a norm in the logical galaxy of morality.

HEDONISTIC WISDOM IN PRACTICE

Granted, then, theoretical legitimacy, the hedonist may teach us something of practical wisdom. On the social and affirmative side, we have already seen that he has an elemental locus for his prize-pole that leaves him in the field of reform after many a more refined theory has been captured by the enemy. We need not emphasize this further, save to remind ourselves that hedonism, slain in many a classroom and abased in many a pulpit, lives still as lustily as ever in the world of men. It is like the hero of a once popular ballad who, though his legs were shot away, fought still upon the stumps. Wherever men suffer pain that is not necessary, or are urged to sacrifice pleasure unnecessarily, there the common-sense of somebody will rise eloquently to ask, Why? It is a hedonistic query, and the world is better off for its insistence.

THE LURE OF THE IMMEDIATE

On the personal side, there is something in the strategy of virtue to be learned from hedonistic hedgings. Pleasure admitted as a good, can nevertheless hardly be denied to be a dangerous good. Men are, as Plato says, "overcome by pleasure." Thinking of its seductiveness, let us revert to what we have called its "lures." There is, first, the lure of the immediate as against the equal claim of the remote. We may insist here upon the qualifying word "equal" with the best of authority behind us. Henry Sidgwick, who spent his life seeking the truth in this field, was driven (*Methods of Ethics*) to a double conclusion: (1) that hedonism must become rational in order to be justifiable, i.e., every unit of pleasure in one's life must be accounted equal with every other in estimating what one ought to do, and (2) that to make one's *future* pleasures, unit for unit, hold their own against the undertow of present pleasures, one must accept an "intuition" which operates categorically to bolster day after to-morrow against the massive advantage of today: *hereafter as such must count for as much as today.* Any barnyard rooster can run riot among the hens, but only man, a rational man, can make to prevail the *greater* pleasure of even himself. In avoiding the first lure, hedonism which starts at a barnyard level of egoism leads one, as it becomes most worthy of man, to the lofty perspective of human rationality. Time, the enemy of impetuosity, becomes through patience the agent of reasonableness. Morality founded on impulse, transcends impulse on its way to maturity. Patience yields perspective, and perspective fulfills patience.

THE LURE OF THE SELFISH

Now, as every moral theory has to contend with an illusion of the differential importance of the immediate (however *good* be defined, the tendency is to find more of it nearest us), so every theory can learn something from the way hedonism tries to bear its cross of time. There is another cross, too, common to every theorist, and the hedonist has left us a legacy of wisdom as to bearing it also. It is what I call "the lure of the selfish." Not merely the good that is *now* but also the good that is *mine* has an advantage in every competition. But it is an unfair competition. Nobody but a weakling would boast of his success in giving candy to a child. Good is good, and so one unit of it is as important as another unit. By this token an equal pleasure of another is as important to the Authentic Hedonist as the same amount of his own pleasure. The noble impartiality of self-preference is not impartial enough for a fully rational hedonist.

HEDONISM TRIUMPHANT OVER DIFFICULTIES

We must state the matter generally, for every moral theory has to contend with a similar foreshortening of perspective, in both social and temporal distance. Hedonism's way of meeting this foreshortening is commendable, though no method is wholly successful in practice. Even such a theory (subsequently to be studied) as holds that the good is Self-Realization must meet the preferred claim of one self as against another important self. Now a certain reference to self is inevitable in every theory. To that extent every act is "selfish"; but there are many kinds of selves; and some of them are as different from others as what is commonly called selfishness is different from unselfishness. The hedonistic way of trying to equalize the pleasure of all selves is to emphasize as source of pleasure a self that understands all this and thus jumps out of its narrow skin, so to say, through a true vision of the equality of all selves.

To resist the lure of the selfish is as important as to resist the lure of the immediate, with which it can become identified and so be doubly strong as an undertow away from rationality. Every moral theory is subject to the attrition of both lures, and the hedonistic method of resistance to this dual attrition is full worthy of praise.

The Good is the Pleasurable, the pleasurable and the more.

CHAPTER 7

THE GOOD AS SELF-REALIZATION

The unfolding logic of the immediately preceding chapter has brought us to a kind of cumulative goal in terms of which to state the Good. *Self-realization,* as the conventional word goes. Let us, now, accept the leading of this logic and see what we can make of the notion that, while pleasure and happiness are elements in goodness, the Good itself is best stated as fulfilment of the capacities of the self. But of what self—and which capacities?

THE GIVEN SELF

Here, through a question as difficult as it is inevitable, we are brought face to face with what in its full reach is a metaphysical undertaking. We cannot avoid it, even though we can here but skirt it. In its consideration we shall meet our theological friends, Kant and Butler—and see now more fully what they mean. It is an old view of the matter that God bequeaths to the organism of man at the proper time—conception, birth, or at some subsequent "age of accountability," or when not—a soul whose vocation on earth is determined by its pre-natal career. If this career somewhere intersects the nefarious path of the devil, then man must "be born again" before he can really overtake his career-line on the earth-pilgrimage. If the soul comes neat from God, with no dalliance along the way, then it needs only to discover its own deeper bent, through conscience or reason a priori, to know what it must fulfill through its functions. Suffice it to say that the theologians, and their closest philosophic allies, have usually taken a dim, yea the very dimmest, view of the soul's dalliance with the devil. And so, as the corrective imps in Kipling's *Tomlinson* reported to his Satanic Majesty—

The soul that he got from God he has bartered clean away.
We have handled him, we have dandled him, we have seared him to the bone,
And sure if tooth and nail show truth he has no soul of his own.

This is the substantial conclusion, even if less sad, to which thinkers have come, through a derivation vastly different from the theological: the conclusion, that is, that man, the animal, "has no soul of his own." Not because he "bartered it clean away," but because he never had any soul. Not with any devil has he dallied, but with a sort of bedevilled evolutionary line, borrowing predispositions along the cosmic route from every layer of his lower kin. Man comes, these say, upon the mundane scene of this "big, boomin', buzzin' confusion" with the undertows of the animal, of the savage, of the semi-civilized barbarian, and of the child. While these tug him backwards if not downward, he is subjected quickly enough, by the development in him of purpose, to goals that beckon him onward if not upward. Through the dynamic multiform of imagination, he is pulled toward any number of potential selves. William James describes this potentiality with humor near kin to pathos: "not that I would not, if I could," said he, "be both handsome and fat and well dressed, and a great athlete, and make a million a year, be a wit, a bon-vivant, and a lady-killer, as well as a philosopher: a philanthropist, statesman, warrior, and African explorer, as well as a 'tone poet' and a saint."

THE EGO-CENTRIC PREDICAMENT IN ETHICS

To whichever of these derivations of the self we incline, there are two aspects of self-realizations which emerge. One we wish immediately to remark, so as henceforth to avoid it; the other we wish presently to clarify so as to turn it to ethical account. The first is, as already suggested, that the self of any given time functions inexorably in whatever we do, and operates to determine morality whether the latter be conceived as of the Right or as of the Good. This is the unavoidably deterministic aspect of the moral life. If we choose pleasure as our good, the (future) pleasure which we are presently choosing will be weighted by the (present) pleasure given us at the thought of the pleasure that is to come. If we are "selfish," the purview of our choice will be narrowed to what selfish men see—and the woe of our choice will be the weight of our egoism. "It is always one's self," writes Sainte-Beuve, "that one loves, even in what one admires." Our future will be caught in the toils of what the past has made our present to be. It is even so with whatever else we choose as our Good. We choose *that* as our good only if we are already the kind of person who is quickened by the contemplation of such an alternative.

In this sense, all men are "selfish"; for the perspective of every man reflects the self of the past and projects that self into the future through the medium of choice. Whether we like it or not, this is inevitable; and it is best to accept the inevitable with natural piety and courtly grace. If we jump from this necessary participation of our selves in all our choices ("the ego-centric predicament" in ethics) to the dogma that, therefore, all choice is trivial, we play with words—and it is a play, too, that obscures rather than clarifies the issue. In the way which it is true, it is trifling to say that all action is selfish; for from the vantage of that ubiquity we must immediately redistinguish between both men and motives in terms of whether, if we may put it so, they are "selfishly" selfish or "unselfishly" so. Admitting, therefore, the fact of the predicament, we refuse to bedevil ourselves with a commitment which obscures from us the issue.

The issue is: What *kind* of a self do we wish to *realize?*

THE GIVEN SELF RELEGATED

What we have been saying of the "ego-centric predicament" applies as much to the god-derived soul of theology as to the purposive self of the evolutionist. If the soul with which we started to earth got corrupted along the path of parturition, then the impure soul we bring into the world colors, and indeed poisons, our every choice. It warps our sense of duty to where, with Faust, we choose the evil to be our good. It is just this fact which makes it imperative that if we be children of the devil, we must be born again before any of our choices, including our very conception of duty, can safely be allowed us.

If we have been born again, or if better still we arrived on earth without some metaphysical "corruption of blood," then the pure predispositions of that fortunate soul will commit us, through inner peace at the thought, to dependable duty in every unfolding choice.

In waiving, then, further preoccupation over the participation inevitably of the self in choice, we relegate to Book I and the Philosophy of the Right, the role of a metaphysically given self. Such a self constitutes a norm *from which* rather than a goal *toward which* purpose inclines and to which choice commits us. In such theories even the self that seems to be chosen as the good is but the projection of a self given by fate, or inevitably determined by the operation of rewards and punishment. Choice itself is more election than selection.

IS NOT THE SELF OF CHOICE ALSO GIVEN?

But is not choice by the evolutionist also a *pre*dilection, as it were, post-maturely coming to cognizance? Only in the sense indicated. Knowing that pleasure of the present self is operative in the prospect of a future self, we are by that understanding, as psychoanalysis implies, given an antidote to inevitability. We can at least put *that* pleasure into a perspective so wide that it must compete with *other* pleasures, including its very opposite, for the favor of an option. This procedure constitutes freedom in a far-reaching sense, the sense of an indefinitely expanding perspective, with proper guards posted at our flanks. One glad fruit of this freedom is that one is not left so often to repent of the choice he has made, in the light of the consequences that follow thereupon. What finer freedom can one have than when fore-sight saves hind-sight from regret?

THE SELF TO BE CREATED THROUGH CHOICE

We recur, then, with minds somewhat cleared, to the previous question: What self is to be launched through choice? Now *whatever* be the self, it becomes the given man's good. Such is a fair statement of the factual basis of an ethics of self-realization. Not only is such a goal implied in other ethical theories; but as a statement of independent fact a man must take himself for better or for worse, willy-nilly. Any self taken to be one's own, *is* one's own good, and for that choice one's only good. If for strategic reasons we let that pass—and it is a presupposed value in this present theory of the Good—we may raise the question previous to it. Which would be best of all the possible selves one might become? That question seems to make sense, all other questions apart. If it does make sense, moreover, it suggests here, as we have glimpsed elsewhere, that Good is not adequately defined by any given quality of the "self." Good appears to be something over and above the self, by knowledge of which we pick the *better* self, just as it appeared to be something independent of pleasure by which we skimmed the cream of pleasure.

This continuously retreating residue will drive us eventually to what many have regarded as a more ultimate and a more objective view of our norm, "Good as good." If "higher" pleasure commits one to something *better* than pleasure itself, by which to make the distinction stick, so a choice between selves commits one to choose the "better" self, even though the price be that the *better* becomes the norm above the self. When the judged becomes the judger, self-realization slips from *the* Good to *a* good, as determined by whatever standard is surreptitiously operative in the premises.

We have already seen how Bentham tried to avoid the surreptitious by denouncing all "quality" of pleasure and by making "better" mean simply *more* of the same, i.e., more *pleasure*. May not the self-realizationist similarly save the integrity of his theory, by lowering his sights? The self to be realized becomes, let us say then, only *more* selves. Or, speaking in the singular, the self to be realized is one that includes in its amplitude the most of all potentialities that can be harmonized by any means of integration at hand. This, then, is the self we shall discuss, leaving what is surplus to it, if anything be, for another theory to appropriate. With the self so conceived, we have at hand in self-realization a moral theory of great value. Let us observe in more detail what its special virtues are.

We have a historic guide to help us along the path we have now chosen. Thomas Hill Green, eminent Oxford don of the 19th century, is our man. He bulked large in his time, and has left a redolent moral memory for our time. He was one of the very few philosophers, if indeed there be any others, who rated the immortality of a novel written around him as its hero. He is the original of Mrs. Humphrey Ward's *Robert Elsmere*. Green's ethical philosophy came close to being the official view the British Empire Builders took of their historic vocation, the better part of the "White Man's Burden." We Americans can afford even a more careful look at Green's philosophy for another reason: John Dewey, the North American pragmatist, took his departure as an ethicist from this Englishman rather than from the German Hegel, to whose general philosophy Dewey (and Green also) were deeply indebted.

T. H. GREEN'S "ABIDING SELF"

T. H. Green, in his famous *Prolegomena to Ethics,* saw that any definition of the self which identified it with any human desire is too narrow; for clearly we require a standard, as we have seen, to help us distinguish between desires that are better and those that are worse. Any actual self would be outmoded at the prime. But Green saw more than this.

He saw that any self identified with *all* desires would also be too narrow as a norm, as of course it would be too wide as to content. Just as a self would burst with a plethora of variety which sought to accommodate all desires, so a self would be too narrow to be its own norm if it confined itself to the field of actual desires. We cannot confine ourselves to any one desire; we cannot satisfy ourselves with all desires. All this Green saw, and still more.

The "more" that he saw, was what we have been saying: that if the self is to judge between desires, it must be above desire. The sum of pleasures, he urged against Bentham, is not a pleasure but a *sum*. So also the judgment upon desires is not a desire but a judgment. Now this is what Kant saw, as we have already discerned. Kant in his rigor made the self the judge; so completely the judge, indeed, that there was nothing worthy for it to adjudge. Kant's judgment becomes a norm without content: the Right as the right, for Right's sake. Kant's self judges empirical content only in the sense of condemning it, excluding it from the moral life. Green we are discussing under the "Ethical as the Good," because Green has a content for his judgment. His theory enfolds a norm but supports a content—and boasts a formula for applying the norm to the content and for accommodating the content to the norm. The *potential* self is the norm, but the desires of the actual self are the contents for its realization.

The Self of Green finds credentials for its claim to tower above its content in the simple fact of its self-consciousness. A part of the world of nature, the self nevertheless *understands* nature. How could we *under*stand nature if we did not *over*shadow nature? We not only understand nature as something objective, we understand ourselves as something subjective. A self that understands its desires is more than its own content. This "more than nature" is the self as *norm;* this "less" than norm is the self as content. There are many "me's"; there is only one "I." The "I" is not only more than any "me"; it is more than all "me's." It can make the many "me's" to be one, because it itself is one.

It is in the oneness of the self that Green hides the magic of the normative. Not only does the individual self give unity to the manifold of its content, but all selves are also one, looking upward; as they make one of the many "me's," looking downward. As self-conscious it transcends its contents, so also it over-passes the finite self; and there arises from this self-transcendence a cosmic Consciousness which is norm to all finite selves, as each finite self is norm to its own plural desires.

Operative, therefore, in our choice between desires is a principle which prescribes to the self adjudging what it shall be. No longer is the self left to levitate from its own bootstraps; it is now lifted from beyond itself by clairvoyance of the Whole which functions as a unity to pull its own parts together in the rationality of selfhood. There is an "abiding self" which moves upon the troubled waters of our many desires to make them one through the transforming power of its own coherence. This "abiding self" has its own unique type of satisfaction.

"THE ABIDING SATISFACTION"

This self gives reality to the potentialities of our own selves. What we call our own unrealized possibilities would be nothing if they were mere possibilities. To make possibilities meaningful, thinks Green, there must be an eternal Self in whose consciousness *our* possibilities are already *actualized*. Such a Self would give meaning to aspiration and would constitute for us a norm to be applied to, but not to be exhausted by, the natural wants which go to make up the contents of our organic selves. The satisfaction which comes from natural wants gratified, is ephemeral, requiring replenishment in endless recurrence. There is no "abiding satisfaction" for such a self. The Eternal Self, on the other side, has satisfactions to match its own nature, "meat to eat ye know not of." Since our human selves partake of both the finite and the infinite, we reach from recurring satisfactions of a changing self toward "an abiding satisfaction of an abiding self." The good is any satisfaction of any self; the ultimate good is the satisfaction of an ultimate self. The *summum bonum* is, in Green's happy phrase, "the abiding satisfaction of an abiding self."

Is it an all-or-none proposition? Are we altogether natural, or completely spiritual; and is the passage from the one to the other cataclysmic, or can it be gradual? It is gradual in form, but cataclysmic in essence. A natural desire can never become a spiritual one by anything more of the natural super-added. Green has a formula which marks the transition, though the formula may be applied to desires without limit. Since what makes us spiritual is self-consciousness transcending the self, the formula has to do with extending the ambit of the conscious self. Any wants we may have for objects are and remain natural events. But any desires we have as spirits are and remain spiritual. But a want which *was* natural may *become* spiritual by the presentation of the want to self-consciousness as being no longer just a "want" but now the *good* of a self-conscious agent. A want becomes moral, in Green's phrase, only when "upon the want there supervenes the presentation of the want by a self-conscious subject to himself, and with it the idea of a self-satisfaction to be attained in the filling of the want."

Once this transforming process is initiated, the growth of the spiritual can proceed apace. Once presented at Court all doors are thereafter opened unto you! The potentialities of such a self-conscious agent are, as we have seen, already actualities in the experience of the eternal Self. These possibilities, which seem to apply to sparate selves, are the same for all selves; for all are actually one in the unity of the Eternal Self. The demand of aspiration is, says Green, "at its lowest . . . some well-being which shall be common to the individual desiring it with others; and only as such does it yield those institutions of the family, the tribe, and the state, which further determine the morality of the individual." That at the lowest. At the highest, says Green, the demand of aspiration becomes "a spiritual activity in which all may partake, and in which all must partake, if it is to amount to a full realization of the faculties of the human soul."

We have now before us perhaps the best answer given by the self-realizational school to the difficult question, "What desires of what self are to be the moral standard?" The answer is: any desire of any self that can be made compatible with the desires of all selves. And this is made meaningful by the presence of one Self which is inclusive of all selves, being itself the Eternal Self. That Self is not exhausted by being made a norm, nor compromised in judging finite desires. Whatever desires can be made a part of self-conscious aim are candidates for ethical honors, and those that can be harmonized with all other selves are become full citizens in the kingdom of the spirit. The norm is not exhausted in being utilized as a standard, but does it not exhaust the subject, emptying him as finite of all individual significance?

JOHN DEWEY TO THE RESCUE OF FINITE SELFHOOD

Such was the fear of one American, John Dewey; and he early engaged himself to rescue finite man from servitude which he thought to be involved in Green's apprenticing man to infinitude. Dewey was at the beginning a disciple of the philosophy of Hegel, the influential German thinker of the 19th century. The American's departure from the camp of metaphysical idealism came, as suggested, through dissatisfaction with the ethical philosophy of Thomas Hill Green. At any rate, Dewey's break in writing came from Green's elevation of the Self, Absolute and Eternal, over finite individualities. Dewey's early articles of protest were against the subordination of human selves to the Absolute Self and against Green's preference for "abiding satisfaction" to recurrent satisfactions in time. Dewey objected at once to metaphysical absolutism and to political conservatism. He turned slowly toward what Peirce and William James had already named Pragmatism, but what he himself came to call Instrumentalism.

The American felt that the price Green paid for an outside norm was too great. A norm transcendent to a given realm of experience may better survive application to that realm; but it also cramps in one way or another the content which is thus ordered from without. Dewey sought an indigenous norm. He still called, he did for long at least still call, his ethical philosophy "self-realization." But it was the realization in time of the finite self. With this our old question recurs: What self? Dewey, like Green, emphasized those tendencies in each self which are compatible with all other selves. But he had abandoned Green's reliance for guaranteeing this commonalty, i.e., timeless actualization of all temporal possibilities. So Dewey had to resort in general to the processes of education, to make men who are born different enough alike at last to beget actual agreement. And for the rest, the politics of compromise must effect under man's management what in Green was made pre-existent under the sovereignty of God. In a word, it is the "social" rather than the Absolute self which insistently Dewey seeks to have realized.

Since, however, the term "social self" implies also an egoistic self, which if existent is likely to give trouble, Dewey and his movement were lucky to have a seminal mind, in that of George Herbert Mead, who sought to show empirically that all finite selves are themselves inherently social. Indeed, Mead's researches and reflections convinced him that selves by their very constitution and nature are social through and through. Born without souls, we achieve selfhood through an integration of the roles that we take in the process of maturation. We become a self by assuming the roles of other selves. The growth of self-consciousness comes through this device of role-taking. Fully grown, the synthesis of this role-taking proclivity yields as core of each man what Mead called a "generalized other." The self is, then, by constitution a "socius." Men cannot avoid the social, for it is in them, moves with them, and *is* them. When what began as an animal calls at last upon himself and finds somebody at home, the animal has become a man. That actual, all things become possible by man's realizing as himself all possibilities of the "others" that are within him.

The Good is the Self-Realizational, the self realized and more.

CHAPTER 8

THE GOOD AS THE ADVENTUROUS

Mr. Herbert Hoover, while President of the United States, once to the Boy Scouts of America bespoke in classic form a classic theme about human nature. "A boy," said he, "is an animal who takes exercise upon every possible occasion." If we extend this to the girl, too—admitting as variation on a common theme that she may be actively anabolic while he is super-actively catabolic—then we have isolated an element in youth, which is also adult material, for a certain type of Ethics of the Good. While the prepotency to action may decline in measure as youth passes into manhood and as manhood slips through maturity into senescence, yet it is clear that when the will to action is wholly over, life itself is fully done—yea, alas, is quite *un*-done.

What most surprises the adult who has passed and has also forgotten his youth is this: that the youth is not only active in general; he is, specifically, out *looking for trouble*. To the adolescent in particular only the humdrum is hideous; only the unexciting palls. The parent who meets head-on the tide of gush-and-go, hoping thus to throw it back, such a parent only transforms the given trouble into double trouble. Sometimes to swim with the tide is not only ease but prudence as well. It is often wisdom to help the trouble-seekers find the kind of trouble which will measurably satisfy without being immeasurably expensive in its subsequent outcome. At the bottom of all, youth is on the grow. Now to grow one must get energy; not only so, he must also give energy. To get and to give; to give what one gets, this is the elemental demand made by life upon life, if out of it a close-woven personality is to come.

That wise modern, to whom frequent repair has been made in this book, has given poignant expression in his maturity to the philosophy of youth. Justice Oliver Wendell Holmes in his letters to Sir Frederick Pollock—

octogenarian to octogenarian—summarizes the wisdom of life as the giving of all you've got. The Holmes who had earlier thought that the only thing better than life is *more* life, holds to the end that the good life is the letting of yourself out to the full of your powers. The pathos of life he sees as the ending of it before you have had a chance to test your full strength. The old, thought the aged Holmes, may well die, and leave in their going no sense of tragedy; but it is pure tragedy for the young to die before they have fully lived. Such is his running comment upon cases. His articulation of the philosophy of it takes the form of saying that "the only meaning of life is the living of life."

With this foreword from two modern actors—Herbert Hoover and Oliver Wendell Holmes—let us now pass to a more systematic exposition of the notion that the Good is the "adventurous."

A WORD ON ARISTOTLE

There are few motifs in the multiple life of man which Aristotle has not touched with light. We have long become used to the thought in this book that every moral philosophy has all moral philosophies in it, so to say. Given a viewpoint, all that is good or right must appear somewhere in the view, or something is wrong with the vantage chosen. Now Aristotle had his point of view, a form of rationalism. This was the vantage from which he tried to do justice to all the content of the good life, making his way from pleasure to contemplation. Truth to tell, Aristotle is singularly fecund in clarifying the core of this chapter—the Good as somehow the adventurous. Though the Greek ends with man as rational, he begins with man as active. He gets from the beginning to the ending by working up from vegetable to animal activity and from animal proclivity to imaginative consummation. Along this ladder he moves with the conviction, if we may say so, that there is more "adventure" in action the more the action is sufficient to itself and the more nearly it can be sustained in its self-sufficiency. Aristotle discerned early, though he does not put it in just these terms, that man's supremely rewarding excitement is of the imagination. In the rational processes themselves there is a pageantry that invests the daily humdrum with a light never seen on land or sea. That man is likest God who has discovered how to sustain the activity of thought upon the objects of thought. The youth who takes to dime novels or to the movies as overtopping in meaning such overt activity as is available to him in his search for adventure, he is in essence a young Aristotle, on the grow—but not likely on that unbalanced diet to become fully grown!

Between these two extremes—the adolescent with the only activity he knows, the sensuous; and Aristotle with the only activity which life had in his experience fully confirmed, the contemplative—there lie progressive stages of interpretation to which Justice Holmes has already called attention in his emphasis upon the Good as the outgoing of one's powers. Let us now round out our thought by fixing attention upon certain of these stages, and by doing it as is our wont through the exposition of philosophers who have already deepened the analysis in our present direction.

WILLIAM JAMES AND RADICAL NOVELTY

Hardly any writer more than William James has done justice to the role of adventure in the motivation of youth, and few more than he have so dignified its function throughout life. There was a buoyancy about him that made one know that the youth in him had never died. Though he made the great abnegation implied in choosing which self he would become of the many selves that solicited him early in life, he never ceased to face the future with roseate faith. Like a soul bent on high adventure, he explored the by-paths as well as mapped the main trail. After twenty-five years as a "psychical researcher," his scrupulosity impelled him to admit that he had found little that was dependable, but his hope still guessed that there *was something there:* "well," as he puts it, "to keep a window open upon that quarter in one's mind."

Religion he likewise investigated in all its pathological as well as its pietistic reaches—*Varieties of Religious Experience*—and he came forth at the end with the conviction that religion itself is the sense of "the something more" in life. The universe itself he conceived as so much a locus of growth that the soul that would truly serve its world must come, put its shoulder to the cosmic wheel, and push to help God in his efforts to budge the recalcitrant cosmos the way it ought to go. Life to him was high adventure from beginning to end, adventure and confidence, as he puts it, that "faith in a fact could help create the fact."

Not only does the worthwhileness of living "depend upon the liver," but with a good liver we can afford to go on just to see what the next morning's headlines will be. "There will be news, there will be news, in heaven," James gleefully used to quote a mystic friend of his as saying.

Meantime on earth, James grieved over the encroachment upon the spirit of individual adventure of the motif of security and over the invasion of the soul's own niche by philosophies of high-geared order and organs of expert routine. He was, as he said:

against bigness and greatness in all their forms, . . . against all big organizations, against all big successes and big results, and in favor of the eternal forces of truth which always work in the individual.

He was for science until science narrowed the universe to a tight determinism, and then James was for "the will to believe" whatever one desperately needed in his business. Where there are two loving souls, even though they be on a lonely rock in the sea, there is ethics; and its "guiding principle is simply this: to satisfy at all times *as many demands as we can."*

Man's "demands" reach into the empyrean, though in James' hands for a reason near the opposite of that usually adduced. Most men seek in religion security, all the way from transcendental fire insurance to mundane peace of mind. James, on the other hand says: "The capacity of the strenuous mood lies so deep down among our natural human possibilities that even if there were no metaphysical or traditional grounds for believing in a God, men would postulate one simply as a pretext for living hard, and getting out of the game of existence its keenest possibilities of zest." From beginning to end William James glorified the adventure of living as the final meaning of the good life. "The strenuous type of character," concludes he, "will on the battlefield of human history always outwear the easy-going type."

Thus James lived: so he died; for, as he said at his death, "There is no conclusion. What has concluded that we might conclude in regard to it?"

Ullman's *The White Tower* generalizes James' moral in a setting that James would have loved, the Alps. Several different nationals, bringing the war to poison the ozone of frozen heights, who are banded together in a joint quest to scale a famous but as yet unclimbed Alpine peak, have discussions as to why men climb mountains. Each has his own reason, in keeping with national characteristics; but the Swiss guide caps them all by announcing that the reason he climbs a mountain is the simple one, that the mountain is *there!*

Not merely mountains had better take warning from men's proclivities to act, to act hazardously. An American soldier in World War II, a young man whom I had known since his childhood, asked me when both of us had been demobilized whether he had not given me a good deal of anxiety at one stage of our occupation of Rome. Not being in the same unit with him, I did not at first get what he meant. He explained: had there not been a good deal of consternation in the Allied Control Commission at one time because of some unidentified plane that flew over the Vatican, putatively an American plane? I recalled that there had been, only to be told by him, laughingly, that the plane was *his*. Eyes open with wonder, I asked why in the world he did it. His answer is hardly more characteristic of youth than testimonial to our present moral philosophy, that of adventure: "I just wanted to see what the Vatican looked like from the air, at night!"

Veritably, James was right in feeling that men need to spend their energies, they want excitement; they require adventure.

THEODORE ROOSEVELT AND THE "STRENUOUS LIFE"

Articulation of this motif, especially in America, has not been confined to the philosophers, not by any means. Men of action have spoken the same lesson more eloquently by what they did than have most philosophers by what they said. Daniel Boone declared what is the chief end of man, writing it in his footprints in endless treks. Sam Houston made it clear when, for the sake of a woman's name, he left the Governorship of Tennessee to go again to live with the Cherokee Indians, on his way to Texas and, as it turned out, to historic fortune. Andrew Jackson wrote it again in action, as has Admiral Byrd in our time. Nor have men of action been lacking at times in words to befit their action. Horace Greeley proclaimed the moral in his famous advice, "Go West, young man." And Theodore Roosevelt, combining the love of action with the phrase appropriate to it, has given us anew in modern times the lure of the "strenuous life."

"We believe," said this Rough Rider, "that men must play fair, but that there must be no shirking, and that success can only come to the player who 'hits the line hard.' " To one of his temperament, it is not enough to qualify one for the good life that he does no wrong, that he stands diffidently and inoffensively on the sidelines of life. "It is the plain duty of every man," he asserts to the contrary, "to see that his rights are respected." And even that is not enough. There is a required thrust outward, as well as an adequate defense inwards. "It is the doer of deeds," declared he, " who actually counts in the battle for life, and not the man who looks on and says how the fight ought to be fought, without himself sharing the stress and danger."

There is more than one dimension of the strenuous life. Some men think strenuously; some love with abandon; some drink hard. There is an *intensive* cultivation of adventure as there is an extensive gesture toward the horizon. We cannot omit from the worthies of the adventurous life, the man Henry David Thoreau. No, nor the woman either, Emily

Dickinson. Connoisseurs both of the inner life, but no kinsmen, either, of "Walter Mitty," these two Americans, in different idioms, have taught us the high thrill of in-living. Thoreau, in Walden Wood. Dickinson in a compass narrower still, just a New England house and garden. They both found the universe full of excitement. "I have travelled a good deal," says Thoreau, adding slyly, *"in Concord!"* Since Thoreau held with his friend and mentor, Emerson, that no one ever brought home the wealth of the Indies, unless he had carried that wealth out with him, this in-dwelling is tell-tale of spiritual profundity. Concord was only a village, but quite big enough to make Thoreau's point, his point that "everywhere, in shops, and offices, and fields, the inhabitants have appeared," as he added, "to be doing penance in a thousand remarkable ways." So indeed with all the ill-wrought world! But why should life be penance anywhere, especially everywhere? It is pusillanimous to dress a princess like a drab! You do not have to get further afield, on the positive side, than the first room of your own imagination to find what life's all about! "It is only in contemplative moments," testifies Santayana, "that life is truly vital." But it is Thoreau who for the moment is our sage, and he in philosophic finality declares: "If you would learn to speak all tongues, and conform to the customs of all nations, if you would travel farther than all travellers, be naturalized in all climes, and cause the Sphinx to dash her head against a stone, ever obey the precept of the old philosopher, and Explore Thyself."

That for Thoreau. And what for Dickinson, whom for the occasion we have yoked with the Sage of Walden? Since it is the poet's privilege through but one scoop of her "narrow hands," as our Emily expresses it, "to gather Paradise," we need to know of her only, as she says, that "I find ecstasy in living; the mere sense of living is enough."

If we begin outward, and come inward, our category changes from adventure to that of contemplation. There is adventure of course in the discovery of the contemplative object, new worlds from out there swinging into our ken here! But if we make the role more passive than active, we pass through the aesthetic ranges of experience into the "divine" conceived not as the source of law and origin of duty but as in the creedal description of man's true end, "to enjoy God forever." Better in Plato perhaps than in Christianity do we get the final end rendered contemplatively. "Platonic Love" is a contemplative relationship with the final manifestation of the Form of the Good, "beauty shining in brightness."

FRIEDRICH NIETZSCHE AND THE HIGH WILL-TO-POWER

To lift the ideal of adventure from our national sector of experience and to give it the philosophical spread which it invites, let us turn for climax to the German prophet of Superman, Friedrich Nietzsche. There are quarrelling cults about him, with many interpretations of the power ideal. The easiest one is hardly adequate, the interpretation of *Übermensch* as embodiment of all that's diabolical, ready to practice upon any and all the weak the ruthlessness which Nietzsche sometimes seems to preach. His type of aristocratic leaning does, however, lend itself to an anti-democratic and indeed to an anti-moral use. Nietzsche was unquestionably against the gentler strains in our Western and Christian culture. He was downright against Christianity, and against the Jews whom he blamed for what the Christian world might well praise them: for the genteel and the humane in our culture. "Everything strong, brave, domineering, and proud has been eliminated. God degenerated to the contradiction of life, instead of being its transfiguration and its eternal *yea!*"

But what Nietzsche is *for* is more important than what he's *against*. He is for the great "Yea-Sayer" to life. As one of Nietzsche's most sympathetic critics has remarked, "Late and slowly the world began, or is beginning to change its mind about 'the anti-antichrist,' and to perceive that he was not merely 'anti'; but that the destroyer of the old tables of values was also a creator of new values. For in Nietzsche, destruction was accompanied by creation, wrath by blessing, and his vehement nay by an equally emphatic yea. His nay was directed at sickness, weakness and decadence, while his yea was for all the healthy instincts slandered and suppressed by the religion and morality up to his day. Nietzsche became the redeemer of these honest and virile instincts, and endeavored to make their corresponding lordly virtues contribute to a great vision which he had of the future."

Unquestionably Nietzsche fell in love with heroism. He saw in man's "will-to-power" the leaven that lends virtue to every ideal, a leaven without which potency suffers enervation. This he thought had happened not only to the heroic virtues but also to the classical ideals of Truth, Beauty, and Goodness. "Only he who altereth," he shrewdly observed in those premises, "remains unalterably mine." Unless an ideal keep adding to itself, it never retains its power. To stop growing is for an ideal to become a dogma for a stultifying cult, and that means to have spirituality done to the death by lethargy.

In the life of the spirit, then, no less than in action, heroism is the thing, and heroism requires prowess. "The aim," as he says, "should be to prepare a transvaluation of values for a particularly strong kind of man, most highly gifted in intellect and will, and, to this end, slowly and cautiously to liberate in him a whole host of slandered instincts, hitherto held in check." In pursuance of this Nietzsche looked forward to the hope, he said, "that life may one day become more evil and more full of suffering than it has ever been."

This heroism comes at length in Nietzsche to take the form of a bold maxim: "Live dangerously." This was the injunction he gave not to all, but to his own. "I am a law only for mine own," spake Zarathustra; "I am not a law for all. He, however, who belongs to me must be strong of bone and light of feet." It becomes the vocation of every heroic-fibered man to over-pass common men. On the negative side, the hero must be able, as we say, "to take it." On the positive side, he must be able to inflict it unflinchingly. But all the while and on both sides he is the mouthpiece of the Everlasting Yea and the nemesis of the Everlasting Nay. He seeks danger out rather than waiting for it to overtake him. He welcomes hardship, rejoices in his stamina to stand hardship, and glories in his strength to overcome. Nietzsche's thought at its simplest is like that of Holmes, with whom we began this chapter, stated by Nietzsche thus: "A living thing seeks above all to discharge its strength." It ends with the glorification, as Nietzsche again puts it, of "the maximum potentiality of the power and splendor of the human species." If we try fairly to combine both aspects, the positive and the negative, we get as the object of the new morality which is beyond the conventional "good and evil" what he puts in these terms: "The object to attain that enormous energy of greatness which can model the man of the future by means of discipline and also by means of the annihilation of millions of the bungled and botched, and which can yet avoid going to ruin at the sight of the suffering created thereby, the like of which has never been seen before."

All this sounds, on the off-side to post-war ears, too much like the concentration camps of the Nazis, those self-boasted super-men of yester-year. Lest, therefore, an ideal which is worthy enough in the abstract should be brought into disrepute by those perversely histrionic, let us return to our own democratic culture, bringing with us the ideal of the good life as one that enshrines the heroic notion of living adventurously.

MONTAGUE AND DEMOCRATIC ADVENTURE

All that is good in Nietzsche for our time and place has better been stated for us by an American believer in the fulness of life. It is Professor

William Pepperell Montague, himself a disciple of William James. Setting himself against all jural ethics, he announces as the only law which the good life brooks this: "the law that there shall be no law." In a little book—*Belief Unbound,* subtitled "A Promethean Religion for the Modern World"—Professor Montague has sung in high key the praises of "taking a chance." But what he asks *for* himself he takes not *from* any man. His is not some high aristocratic prowess for which others pay. Montague sees, rather, how open the skies of opportunity are for all, be men but trained to look upward and to embrace the expansive element. "Life," as he summarizes, "is essentially an adventure." He sees that the demand of our day is not less of "the old-time courage of the heart" but certainly more of "the new courage of the mind, the resoluteness to use intelligence to the limit in all dealings with our physical environment, our social institutions, and our own inmost selves."

But to come somewhat more systematically to the moral philosophy of this robust modern, let us observe that he holds two virtues to be primary in the life of adventure: courage and enthusiasm. Courage, one of the oldest prized and always deserving virtues, has been strangely lacking in proper emphasis from ethicists. It needs re-definition, as above, and restoration to a central place. Though life is inherently an adventure, morality has too often concerned itself with the semblances of respectability, with duties that negate every adventurous prompting. Even where a duty-ethics has arisen above parochial inhibitions, as in Kant, it has sought its genius in "the law that there shall be law." According to Montague, as already suggested, the genius of morality lies precisely in the opposite direction . . . "always a departure from law, a maximum of variation, innovation, and adventure."

It is a slave morality that prescribes, "Nay, everlastingly nay," even as Nietzsche thought. Jesus and Buddha, says Montague, had "courage of the heart," capacity, that is, to endure. We must have more than that. We must overcome the undertow toward temperance, never a virtue, says Montague, save in dealing with "our sins and sorrows." "The notion that Temperance possesses intrinsic value," declares Montague, "is as false as it is ancient and as mischievous as it is respectable." Who wants to be, or ought to be, temperate in his joys?

The exact opposite is the lead proposed by Montague in the name of high courage. And here this basic virtue passes easily into what he calls its genius, but what is also clearly its fulfilment. For the greatest virtue is enthusiasm—"all that makes for the hard work of actualizing potentialities." On the analogy of an economic law of diminishing returns Montague enunciates for life and mortals what he calls "The law of Increasing

Returns." This is but his way of dramatizing the truth that good and evil gain by concentration and lose by dispersion. Evils should, it follows, be scattered as much as possible, as, for instance, we do through insurance. But goods should be concentrated as much as possible, even, he suggests, to perhaps the point of well-managed lotteries. Here somebody gets a huge return from trivial investments by the many. At any rate, Montague feels certain that, as he says, "a single beauty is worth more than many pretties; a major poet is worth more than his own weight of minor poets; a supreme ecstasy cannot be equalled by any number of little joys."

This in no sense spells out the cruelty betokened by Nietzsche's hard words, "The misfortunes of all these small folk do not together constitute a sum-total except in the feelings of mighty men." Quite to the contrary, Montague deplores the failure of Christianity to match Buddhism in its mercy toward the lower animals along with humble men. "The howling of a single lost dog on a city street" would impugn the integrity of the mightiest God who claimed to be good, if he had the power but lacked the will to prevent such canine anguish. "We happy and successful members of the conquering race forget that this mountain on which we live is a mountain of skulls, and that the failures, deaths, and miseries of our humbler brethren make up the purchase price of our estate."

No, this doctrine of Montague's is not some overt or covert cruelty; but it is a generalization for all men alike of an ethics oriented toward the adventurous. "To achieve happiness," he cries out, "enthusiasm in the sense of abandon or concentrated intensity should replace temperance as the rule of virtue and true wisdom." Here is at last a philosopher who, in no reckless mood or cruel tense, but merely in the interest of making life what, under God, it ought to be and could be for all men, urges us *to go the limit*—and to do it in the name of a superior ethics. Who since William James has sounded a tocsin note save on behalf of caution? Montague pipes only for the fuller life. "The rewards of 'plunging,' 'going the limit,' 'draining the cup to the last drop,' etc., are out of all proportion greater than those of safe half-hearted dabbling on the principle of nothing too much." This is in Montague's opinion the only attitude, that of unleashed enthusiasm, which is likely, as he feelingly puts it, "to burn away the futilities, frivolities, and wastes that plague us today."

What Montague has thus both preached and practiced as individual virtue, he has also advised in his social philosophy for a bellicose age. In a memorable address before the Seventh International Congress of Philosophy, in Prague, before the Second World War—where Montague also sponsored against the Nazis a ringing declaration in behalf of freedom of speech and conscience—Montague voiced a vision of experimental peace to forestall the war of ideologies. Observing that there are at least two types of men, which of our own accord we may call the dynamic and the sedentary, he proposed a duplex social organization to house these two human types alongside. If they could exist side by side in each country, they might eventually either demonstrate the superiority of one type of organization to the other or confirm the possibility of a political dualism as the permanent variety of economic organization.

Nowhere more than in things social and political is mankind in need of creative imagination. We go on with recurring wars that almost nobody wants but which nobody is inventive enough to see how to prevent. Such audacity as Montague's is the first requirement of statesmanship if the winning of war is not to guarantee the losing of what war is fought to secure. Along the whole front Montague's cardinal virtues shine forth: enthusiasm to invent, courage to perpetrate. Not only in personal life, nor alone in things international. But along the whole metaphysical front, Montague's world is stirred by danger, to be met in mood adventurous. God, freedom, immortality—these things are to him glorious possibilities: *may-be's* that *might be!* The enthusiasm with which Montague has turned his fertile mind to any and every such cause has reduced the amount of lukewarmness in American philosophy. What live man would not, after listening to Montague, would not indeed prefer a probability embraced with enthusiasm to a practical certainty weakly voiced? Religion, for instance, bodies forth, or obscures, what Montague regards as humanity's greatest goods. To this indeed, yea to this in particular, he brings, like his master James, the saving grace of high adventure. "Taking religion as we took it," he concludes one discussion of the subject, "we see at once that it is neither certainly and obviously true nor certainly and obviously false, but possibly true, and, if true, tremendously exciting." Montague advocates for peace as Napoleon advocated in war: "When one can use the thunderbolt, it should be preferred to the cannon."

The Good is the Adventurous, the adventurous and more.

CHAPTER 9

THE GOOD AS THE GOOD

We have now scouted the field of the Good from a number of points of view. Each of these vantages we have found to be rewarding, in that each threw light upon the nature of the moral life in its teleological mode. Clearly no theory has as yet exhausted our subject. If any one theory were wholly adequate, then no other theory would be tenable. We have found them all tenable, and all fruitful, with no one final. The good is what each theory says it is—that, and more. The Good is all its manifestations in turn. As it is clearly more than any, so also it may prove more than all that we have yet thought of. It is not improbable that there is more in the heaven and earth of morality than can be dreamed of in any ethicist's philosophy. I have a surmise that this is what made Plato's lost lecture on the Good so famous: that he said that the Good is all that men have thought it, and more than all that ever would be thought.

There is another possibility little short of scandalous to the simple-minded: the Good may not be complete harmony. If for a fact all the goods together, known and unknown, do not go *together,* then the final good—the ancient honorific, *Summum Bonum*—may have to include whatever relationships the Good-as-Many does exemplify among its members and whatever further relation that manifold has to the Good-as-One. It is not impossible that *the* Good may have to appear as complicated in theory as it is manifold in the practice of the magnanimous, including or even emphasizing the yearning of the Good to be One. The final tribute to the notion that the good is creative would be the discovery that *the Good* is never complete until it is loved by good men.

At any rate, the complication of having on our hands at the end of our discussion more than we had at the beginning seems honorable enough to the fecundity of our subject to justify our calling for time out, a

moment to enjoy as a breathing spell. Let us rest temporarily upon the
security of this truism: *the Good is the Good*. That sounds safe for a
secure breath, even if not forever. For the nonce, then, the Good *is* the
Good. Is it not?

Yes, it *is*.

But why all the to-do about it: why the parrying? Why the scurry-
ing to and fro: the assertion, the iteration, the reiteration? If we're going
to stop with a truism, can we not let it be truistic? Why can we not
let good-enough alone? The reason is that assurance which comes from
re-assurance is never reassuring for long: it carries the seeds of its own
dissolution. The bark that is driven to the isles of the truistic for safety
is soon driven off, by the same wind that brought it to shore. This is the
wind of curiosity, a wind that may die down for a brief spell but never
quite cease to stir in our human embers.

What, for instance, is the *nature* of this Good which *is* just the Good
—and not another thing? Is it an entity, with Plato: some pattern visible
(to the mind's eye), "laid up in heaven," as it were, "which we may
behold; and beholding, organize our lives accordingly?" Is it a *quality,*
with G. E. Moore, in the influential book—*Principia Ethica*—a quality
like "yellow," distinguishable but indefinable? Or is it, as we shall later
ask, a *relation?*

Once curiosity has revived from its fatigue, fidgeting on a truism, the
old questioning begins again. But it begins after wholesome rest, like work
full of cheer following a vacation. The Good is of course the Good; but
not all its devotees agree as to the *nature* of the uniqueness upon whose
existence they have thus agreed. G. E. Moore, who has done most in
our time to *assert* this uniqueness has done little to *establish* it. Indeed
he seems unable to keep himself convinced as to what he believes about
the Good. It is nothing to us at this elementary stage of our ethical investigation but it may yield us a later moral that after proving the Good
indefinable, Moore later declared that all his "supposed proofs were certainly fallacious"; and he went on to say: "I think perhaps [the Good]
is definable: I do not know. But I also still think that very likely it is
indefinable."

For all his honest-minded vacillation about certain aspects of the Good,
Moore has left us in his debt. The first important thing we learn from
Moore is that we know so little about this quality of the Good that we
can safely say that they are wrong who think they know it all. Wrong
they are, for instance, who say of the Good that "nothing but pleasure
is good," or those who say that the good is "only the desired." Such
presumption of knowledge has only for its pains that it has committed

what he calls "the naturalistic fallacy." Such reasoning has, that is, tried to define the undefinable by identifying it with some quality that is "natural"—the "desired" or the "pleasurable." And in the same vein, but at another level, we know so little about this indefinable that we can say that they are also wrong who would up-grade this undefinable quality to a transcendental level and would there identify it with some theological or metaphysical somewhat: with the will of God, for instance, or with some eternal essence. They have for their pains, too, the guilt of another fallacy, what Moore calls "the metaphysical fallacy." Such is, so to say, what we learn *in excess,* from those presumptuous enough to insist upon monopolizing the definition of what is most likely indefinable.

In defect also we have our lesson from equally erring philosophers. There are those who, because the good is simple, think it comes only in singularity. Truth to tell, what is good-in-itself can be identified only in isolation. The "intrinsic good" is that which loses no iota of its virtue even when it "exists quite alone." But it never does as a matter of fact exist alone. It is a fallacy to believe that the simple and the undefinable good, which must be tested by conceiving it quite alone, can ever be as good when alone as when accompanied. There is a positive principle—that of "organic unities"—which to overlook is to commit still another fallacy. The truth is, as Moore conceives it, that no good is so good alone that it would not be better if not alone. A good combined with another good may be better than either alone. A good combined with something neither good nor bad may be better than when alone. Yea, a good combined with an evil may not only make the evil less bad but the good also more good. If this seems curious, it is not for that reason eccentric; it issues, indeed, in a doctrine more piquant still. The doctrine is that already referred to, the Doctrine of Organic Unity, which Moore formulates thus: *"The value of a whole must not be assumed to be the same as the sum of the values of its parts."*

If that seems a great deal to know about this thing so simple and esoteric as to be completely indefinable, then there is more in store. The "more" is this, as finally crystallized by our ethicist: *"The value of a whole bears no regular proportion to the sum of the values of its parts."* Now from this vast imprecision of knowledge Moore draws, in all boldness, one vast conclusion of ignorance as to duty. It is this: that since only wholes have maximum value and since, not knowing the relation between the parts and the whole, we can never know the value of the wholes, then we can never know what our duty is. He puts it even stronger: "we never have any reason to suppose that an action is our duty; we can never be sure that any action will produce the greatest value possible." This conclusion would seem to be justified not only, as Moore justifies it, in terms of "the inadequacy of our causal knowledge," but also in terms of the impossibility of our knowing the value of wholes because we can infer nothing about that value from the relation to it of the parts of it. Or is there, in fact, some esoteric way of knowing wholes whose values are incommensurate with that of their parts?

Now this question provokes a previous question, in a general form: the question as to how Moore knows all this anyhow—all this, I mean, about the fallacies of others and all this about the certainties of himself. A moralist who makes it his business to put others right is inviting any and all to set him right. "With what measure ye mete, it shall be measured to you again."

If Moore has a way of knowing that good is so simple as to be indefinable, then why can he not know in the same direct manner the value of wholes themselves? And if the value of some wholes, then why not the value of those wholes that count for most in human life, the wholes to which we pay deference in acknowledging and in doing our duty? Why does Moore, that is, fail of speculative coherence (he fails not of the customary type) between his teleological ethics and the jural aspects, since, as we have seen from the beginning, the moral life involves both the Right and the Good?

Every moral theory, like every kind of theory, subjects itself at any time to confrontation with the question: How do you know what you are now saying? "Criticism," wrote Sainte-Beuve, "is . . . a perpetual *creation*." We are driven to this previous question particularly as concerning Moore, both by his sharpness toward other moralists and by the agnostic nature of his conclusion regarding duty (agnostic only as to the *knowing* of duty; the *doing* is simplified by his reducing duty to custom).

INTUITION AND ETHICAL ASSURANCE

Though G. E. Moore is one of the sharpest critics of intuitional ethics, his final reliance for the kind of knowledge of the good we have been discussing, is upon intuition. He dismisses almost disdainfully all historic forms of intuition, but then relies wholly upon a form of his own. To make this clear will yield us a closing example of the good-as-good, and will at the same time advance us upon our way to a final affirmation. The truth is that intuition is the chief reliance of every moralist. By this we mean simply, to begin with, that we can know things ethical, as we know other things, by merely meeting with them and seeing that they are so. *Certain* ethical things, we had better qualify ourselves to say. And *what* ethical things are these?

It is the type of ethical certainties, as well as the number of them, claimed by other moralists that makes a critic like Moore cautious, perhaps even over-cautious. Look at a few examples that justify caution. The Professor of Theology at Padua, for instance, claimed to Galileo that he could know without looking that what Galileo said he discerned through the telescope was not there. Or, if it was there, it was extemporized by the devil, to beguile souls predisposed to sin! Wrote Galileo: "Oh, my dear Kepler, how I wish that we could have one hearty laugh together at this glorious folly!" But it is no laughing matter to the convinced, nor yet to those whom they convict upon an intuition—not even to Galileo in the end! Cromwell was reduced, in meeting those whose intuition would have bankrupted his program, to an appeal: "By the bowels of Christ, I beseech ye bethink you that you may be mistaken!" John Cotton, the American Puritan, saw, simply saw by way of routine inspection, that Roger Williams, for all his self-seeming honesty, "suffereth not for his conscience, but by his sinning against his conscience"—and out went Roger Williams on his ear, and that in the dead of winter! Intuition, buttressed with power, is ever the citadel of persecution. But why extend the list? The roll-call of conscience itself, honor-roll as it is to the like-minded, is but the roster of iniquity, the tocsin of sadism, to those who suffer from its "certainty."

Moore is aware of all this, in the annals of action. What is more, he is aware of it in the history of moral theory. He saw how Kant elevated something like intuition into a defense of what some, Moore included, have deplored as a dogma. He saw how Butler had defended conscience as the comrade of reason and the voice of deity, not to be put by. He saw how More, through the designation of "a boniform faculty," had managed to prove good whatever in advance he felt to be good. Moore was warned by the practice of the intuitionists—he thought the *mal*practice—warned to beware of intuitionism as designative of duties. The only safety in intuition as a method of determining duty is to pluralize its poison. When equally self-evident "duties" begin to cancel each other out, then a method, another method than intuition, must be found for making intuitions safe for morality, compatible with civilized tolerance. It is a man's obligation, in a civilized world, to act in such fashion as to produce the maximum amount of good. But no man can know what that action is for certain; it involves the future, which is unknown, and it involves the consequences of consequences, which can never, can never

yet, be completely tabulated. To settle the dubious by drawing the sem-
blance of premature certainty about it, only transforms personal nervous-
ness into social invidiousness. So Moore, out of historically engendered
caution, was driven to refuse to dogmatism the fair mantle of self-decep-
tion. Intuition has often been but the short-cut to certainty which isn't
there. "It is plain," declares Moore with finality, "that no moral law is
self-evident."

That is the locus of Moore's historic deviation: Qualities may be in-
tuited; laws never, the Good, yes—the Right, no. Such a distinction is
safe, but it is not satisfactory to most men. Qualities may be there to be
known, but they are not there to be obeyed. Men want to obey. Or, at
least, they want to know with as much certainty as possible what ought
to be done; and if this obligation comes in the form of a demand (it
might be from within as well as from without), it appears the more un-
ambiguous. What drives men to a doctrine of intuition at all, is likely
to drive them on past qualities and entities into the embrace of "categorical imperatives." It is possible that Matthew Arnold's lines describe man,
in this regard, as he is, but not, I think, as man would like to be:

> We do not what we ought,
>   What we ought not, we do,
> And lean upon the thought
>   That Chance will bring us through.

Men, I am convinced, want as little "chance" as possible in their moral
enterprise. There have been other wise men besides Moore who have
warned that it's better "not to know so much than to know so much that
ain't so." Mere private *certitudes* do not pan out well when treated as
logical certainties. To quote Holmes again: "No statement of fact is ever
self-evident."

Moore's opposition to the certification of laws and principles by intuition is, therefore, understandable; and most men of the world will
applaud it. They have seen the damage done by bogus certainty. But
Moore goes so far as to leave himself high and dry about any and every
duty (save only as he equates duty with custom). Why, to be specific, was
Moore moved to deny intuitive knowledge of the goodness of organic
unities, where reside the greatest values? Driven to it in part, no doubt,
by the fact that obligations are themselves among the chief organic unities
of value, he did not wish, back-handedly, to invest obligation with pseudo-
certainty. But there are organic unities short of obligations. Friendship
is one. Love is another. Aesthetic contemplation is still another. These,
indeed, Moore himself mentions and praises as among the greatest value
aggregations. How does he know that, which is to say how does he recog-

nize these complex experiences as among the greatest intrinsic goods? He seems to recognize not *them,* but it—"it" being in this case the simple quality of goodness. *They* are merely where *it* resides. He finds it among them, recognizes it for what it is. But it is *more* in this setting than in another setting. The "more" he also recognizes, and apparently recognizes intuitively. There may be grave difficulty here, arising from identifying the good with a quality that waxes and wanes with its setting; but we pass it for the moment to pursue Moore's main motif to its conclusion.

That main motif is the intuitive knowledge we actually have of this quality of goodness, but of it alone. Of it in its setting, yes; but not of the setting which swells it from mere existence to maximum meaning. As to knowledge of the simple quality itself, then, we have the answer to our previous question: Moore knows the quality of goodness, and knows it by "intuition." To say that it is indefinable is by no means to hold it unknowable. It is, rather, to hold it knowable by inspection, not by analysis. "It is one of those innumerable objects of thought," he says specifically, "which are themselves incapable of definition, because they are the ultimate terms by reference to which whatever is capable of definition must be defined." The reason indeed why we cannot define it, in the ordinary sense of that term, is that we know it too well—know it as the "simple" thing it is; and so we cannot break it up into parts-it-does-not-have, in order to exhibit its composition. Its evidence is its essence, and that is all there is to it. We know but cannot tell, for there is nothing to tell *about* it, save that we saw it, and nothing to tell this nothing *with,* save the wag of the finger that locates it. "There it is," says the finger eloquently; "that's what I mean by goodness!"

Now Moore has his own explanation of all this, and he is entitled to be heard. After he is heard, his famous teacher is entitled to be heard; for this eminent tutor, Henry Sidgwick, rounds out the doctrine of Intuitionism in its full historic form. While we are at it, we should finish our account, remembering that reliance upon intuitive knowledge characterizes the doctrine that Right is Right, quite as much as we are now finding it to underlie the doctrine that Good is Good. We expect to make use of this commonalty in displaying, in our next chapter, the meeting ground between these two extremes.

LEVELS OF INTUITIONISM

We know, then, says Moore, the simple quality of goodness, by intuition. We do not know, says he, and we cannot know, says he, the complex, the causal, material of obligation, not by intuition. This potency and this impotency seem equally plain to Moore. What is not plain, not made plain to me at least, is how we know the more important intermediate realm of value entities, "the organic unities," in which alone reside the maxima of the quality goodness. Moore does not seem to treat this matter adequately, though one would think it stands in desperate need of clarification if not indeed of certification. True, he speaks of these intermediate value maxima with the same assurance as he speaks of goodness itself. And it may be that he assumes that what he seems to know so satisfactorily is known by the method itself most dependable. It is a hazardous assumption in the light of the reasons, including his own reasons, for denying intuitive certainty to assertions of duty. There have been moralists to assert that while we can never know what is good, we can find out what our duty is. Moore is not without opinions upon this moot point. "It is the essence of Intuitionism," says he, "to suppose that rules of action—statements not of what ought to *be,* but of what we ought to *do*—are in the same sense intuitively certain." Moore admits that "we are . . . often intuitively certain of our duty, *in a psychological sense.*" He means, not that we have "certainty," but only *certitude,* which is a vastly different matter. The reason that we have only "psychological" assurance about judgments of obligation is that "they are capable of being confirmed or refuted by an investigation of causes and effects" (save only that our ignorance forbids!). He does not deny that we *seem* to have intuitions of causal events, nor that these seeming-intuitions may at times be true; but he affirms that "since *what* we intuit, *what* conscience tells us, is that certain actions will always produce the greatest sum of good possible under the circumstances, it is plain that reasons can be given, which will shew the deliverances of conscience to be true or false" (excepting, again, our ignorance of the complete causal sequence, and that through all time!).

HENRY SIDGWICK AND GENERAL INTUITIONISM

On that latter point, Moore is accurate. What he claims may be all that a *utilitarian* conscience would think to tell us, i.e., that certain actions will produce the best consequences. There *are* consciences, to the contrary, which claim to discern that certain actions are right regardless of consequences, *right in themselves.* While to treat this claim here violates our general division of labor—it reverts to the doctrines concerning Right, of Part One—it is fruitful to bring the matter to the present fore in order to prepare for our next chapter, in which the Right and the Good are to be brought as close together as respect for the facts allows.

Moreover, no more certainty seems to attend Moore's consciousness of the quality "good" than appeared to attend Kant's consciousness of the Categorical Imperative.

Now it was Moore's famous teacher, Sidgwick, who slowly became aware of this, and did most about it. What he did, first, was to make clear the complexity and spread of the whole intuitional claim in the moral field. He initially distinguishes what he calls "Perceptional Intuitionism." This is well beyond the kind which Moore has been claiming: it is a direct approach through perception to what is nevertheless obligatory. Then there is, in Sidgwick's term, "Dogmatic Intuitionism." This is the claim that one can see judgments of hortatory fact, general prescriptions of duty, see them to be certainly true. This is the type of claim that Moore has been at greatest pains to deny. It is indeed the type of moral presumption that has been most responsible for the practice of intolerance and most to blame for the bad name of morality among magnanimous men. Yet it is difficult on any ordinary ground to deny that fanatical men see, as intuitively evident, the fact that they ought to persecute others. "If you have no doubt of your premises or your power," says Justice Holmes . . . "you naturally sweep away all opposition. . . . Persecution for the expression of opinion seems to me perfectly logical." Finally, Sidgwick distinguishes what he calls "Philosophical Intuitionism," of which more in a moment. Sidgwick is prepared to admit "Perceptional Intuitionism," without stressing it. He is energetic to deny "Dogmatic Intuitionism." He is chiefly concerned, however, to prove "Philosophical Intuitionism."

Sidgwick's life work was in fact in support of this latter claim, "Philosophical Intuitionism," namely, that there are discoverable a few fundamental principles in the moral field which furnish to ethics the same sort of solid underpinning that axioms provide for geometry. They are not so much duties—certainly not in the dogmatic sense—as they are attitudes which condition all effective duties. After searching the Western World over, ransacking alike the basements of the Common Law and the attics of Christian faith, Sidgwick thinks that he finds three such propositions as will stand the light of critical day. The one prescribes the attitude of Benevolence: that normally other men are entitled to equal consideration with ourselves. The other, as comfortably as surprisingly, countenances the attitude of Egoism: that every man is entitled to look after his own interests. The third proposition prescribes Justice: that, since Egoism and Benevolence are sometimes at outs, we are not entitled to make distinction between ourselves and others, except upon the showing of actual and concrete differences between us. As a rule of choice, no "noble impartiality of self-preference."

Sidgwick not only winnows these out with the greatest threshing pains, but he also subjects them, successfully he thinks, to four rules which he bequeaths to safeguard the truly "intuitional" against ever lurking prematurities. These rules to determine fairly what is intuitively valid follow:

    I. The terms of the proposition must be clear and precise.
   II. The self-evidence of the proposition must be ascertained by careful reflection.
  III. The propositions . . . must be mutually consistent.
  IV. Since it is implied in the very notion of Truth that it is essentially the same for all minds, the denial by another of a proposition that I have affirmed has a tendency to impair my confidence in its validity.

We pass by the uncomforting fact, of Proposition II, that intuition is not a substitute for hard work, and by the suspicious fact, of Rule III, that Sidgwick's "Benevolence" and "Egoism" are sometimes at war; and we pass by the distressing fact that Moore's downright denial of the self-evidence of *any* proposition about duty at all must have (Rule IV) weakened Sidgwick's confidence in his results. We pass these by in order to hazard the larger indictment: that appeal to intuition yields certainty only where it is least needed, and fails to yield it where it is most needed. Assertions of certainty never allay doubts, not for long at least. When doubt arises, intuition does not allay; it but intensifies argument between those equally—and *intuitively*—certain.

We admit that *Good is Good,* as we have earlier admitted that *Right is Right.* We admit both; but, admitting them, we declare that what that tells us about either Right or Good is far short of what we wish to know, and need to know. All moralists resort to intuition, as most of them appeal to it. But what everybody does to nobody's satisfaction is hardly sufficient grounds to support a definitive ethics. Intuition confirms only like-mindedness. Unlike-mindedness, composed of sterner stuff, must be met by sterner methods. Harmony is not established by intuition. Certitude that flourishes in the face of forthright denial is a doubtful virtue, save to the vicious, save to the fanatical. All ethics begins with something intuitive, but no magnanimous ethics can end with that. Where antithetical views are equally intuitive, we have too much intuition, not too little. We require either an intuition, which will settle the opposition among the intuitive, or something with which to pick the truly intuitive. The Good *is* the Good.

    What then?

BOOK III

THE MORAL LIFE AS SYNTHESIS

We have now considered the moral as both the Right and the Good. We have seen the spread of each concept. And while we now discern, as we earlier guessed, that the right is the right and the good is the good, we now know much more about both than the mere intuition of self-identity. We know much better than we knew before that though right is Right, morality is not merely rightness: that though good is Good, morality is not merely goodness.

We see fruitfully what all along we glimpsed abstractly, that morality is a synthesis of the Right and the Good, of the Good and the Right. What the principle of this synthesis is, is as yet undetermined. Those who begin with the importance of the Right are not privileged to stop until they find and accommodate goodness; nor can those who seek the Good ignore duty or neglect the notion of rightness. They must insist, having found rightness, upon doing justice to it under the aegis of the concept with which they began.

Without pressing at this point the principle of these alternative subordinations, we can body forth in general the shape which the total process takes. Beginning with Rightness as the key ethical concept, good becomes descriptive either of the Will from which duty issues, or the name for the increment, unearned it may be on earth, which will yet reward the performance of duty. Good, in short, becomes the bouquet of duty: those rightly good getting the goods. Beginning with goodness, duty becomes a means to its maximization. It is always and everywhere the duty of one who is right to perform the act which of all possibilities will produce the most goodness.

It is now our concluding privilege to spell out the fuller meaning of the moral by seeing in detail how the two points of view conspire to that synthesis which matures into the philosophy of life of the well integrated personality.

CHAPTER 10

THE MEETING OF EXTREMES: THE RIGHT AND THE GOOD

We have often been reminded through foregoing chapters that while the distinction between the Right and the Good is convenient, it is far from absolute. We have thought it wise to dramatize the distinction, because life itself so often and so tragically differentiates these concepts. But we have never been in doubt that the task of the moral life is to get them together, as quickly and as securely as possible. Not two kinds of ethics, therefore, but two points of view—the jural and the teleological—have informed the organization of this book. If we now make a concerted drive to bring these dissidents together in a common fruitage, we shall but be fulfilling the deference each theory pays the other, while at the same time be furthering our aspiration to display the human vocation as One Life for each individual. "The real sin," says a psychoanalytic poet, "consists in being divided against oneself—in wanting one thing but doing another."

The witness readiest at hand to this ethical unity is found in the common reliance of both points of view upon intuitionism as a method. Let us say now, as we have hitherto only suggested, that Henry Sidgwick thought to demonstrate that the Right and the Good actually meet in the shared need for and the common use of the intuitional method. Himself initially a disciple of Utilitarianism, the doctrine of the Good which has been historically most antithetical to all intuitions of Right and Duty, Sidgwick became progressively convinced that, though Utilitarianism scouted intuition, it itself had no firm foundation save in intuitive knowledge. And, strangely enough, the intuition which Sidgwick found John Stuart Mill's doctrine of the Good to be most desperately in need of is the very insight which Kant, connoisseur of the Right, had also sought to derive intuitively, or, as Kant would say, *a priori.*

Specifically, Sidgwick discovered that the Bentham-and-Mill *pleasure* philosophy required in a pinch that men should be willing to sacrifice purely "selfish" pleasure to "the greatest good of the greatest number, each to count for one and nobody for more than one." That such sacrifice might be practically necessary was clear but that it is rational for an egoist to have to act the part of the altruist was not so clear. In deference to necessity, however, Bentham set his "sanctions" like a policeman to guard the gates, and Mill advised a generous resolution of the conflict. Said Sidgwick, however: "I put aside Mill's phrases that such sacrifice was 'heroic'. . . . I knew that any rate I was not the kind of moral hero who does this without reason; from blind habit. Nor did I even wish to be that kind of hero. For it seemed to me that that kind of hero, however admirable, was certainly not a philosopher." It is more ignoble for a philosopher to act rightly with no reasons than for him to act wrongly with right reasons. What would make it rational for a man to do that which is odious but is still necessary for him to do? The answer to that is precisely what Sidgwick discovered: an intuitive obligation, self-evidently binding him as a rationl being to such action. Not only did the intuitions of Justice and Benevolence thus instate the crucial insight of Kantian ethics as foundational for Utilitarian ethics, but another intuition—the Maxim of Prudence—was found necessary to make even Egoism rational. Though slightly afield, this we should also spell out before going on to detail how this conspicuous ethics of the Good had to include the Right in order to fulfill its own vocation.

Egotism is one thing, *egoism* is another. One may, if he be close enough to the animal order, simply announce that he is going to have his way, and then push brutally to get it. Unreflective self-assertion is sometimes observed, but is everywhere deplored among civilized people. Its practice belittles intelligence, even if it be perfectly unconscious, and be in that sense innocent of morality. Intelligent people, even though selfish, must pursue a present good with some reference to its fruitage. This requires perspective, a virtue which the term egotism does not clearly betoken. Egoism does. When one sees that his future good merits the same estimation as his present good, and then proceeds to concern himself about it, he has become rational. His egotism levels out to egoism through the discipline of Prudence. Such perspective does not grow wild on trees, however. I speak of it as a discipline: it has to be learned and paid for. Selfishness pays off only when enlightened, with some intuitive appropriation of perspective.

Even though Sidgwick's claim be true that intuitionism is shared by all schools, trouble remains. If true, it is so generally true that it is hard to infer anything specifically from it. What is true for all theories—intuition as a method, for instance—is not distinctly true of any. No advantage can be derived from the doctrine save the over-all advantage of showing that all theories have something in common. But commonalty need not be ameliorative. The ubiquitous is not invidious. The fact, if it be a fact, that they proceed from a common source, however, is not as significant as that they proceed toward a common goal. Regardless of a neat derivation from a common intuitive source, altruism and egoism still are frequently in conflict, as though they had never met and engaged themselves to unity on their way up from the intuitive primordial. If the fact that they inconveniently conflict, however, drives men to devise ways and means of getting them together in the end, this is of constructive significance. Now such is the case. And in the light of it, we prefer to place our heaviest stake upon this outcome.

The truth is that no theory of the Good can rest content until it has included the Right, nor any theory of Right until it has become also the Good. Let us now make this clear from each point of view.

AFFINITY OF THE GOOD FOR THE RIGHT

This same Utilitarianism of which we have been speaking, long before it culminated through Sidgwick in a source-unity with the Right of Kantianism, was feeling its way to a more satisfactory resolution of the claims of the opposing point of view. Let us not under-estimate the distance it had to go. It was one of the most bellicose forms of ethical teleology. It arose in a world where, juristically, politically, and religiously speaking, the Right embodied what the Utilitarians regarded as extreme wrong. Bentham's situation, for instance, was almost precisely the same as that described in America later by Thoreau: "The greater part of what my neighbors call good I believe in my heart to be bad, and if I repent of anything, it is very likely to be my good behavior." Since what holy men called the Will of God, what legislators denominated as Right, juristic agents of the state described as Justice, since these forms of the Right were all almost altogether bad, Bentham got a simple definition of the Good and set out to overthrow its antithesis.

He had of course his own definition of Right. But it was a definition based upon the Good. That conduct is right which maximizes the Good; wrong which does not minimize the bad. Pain is bad, and anybody can know with much certainty when he is suffering. Nor can others easily deny that one is suffering pain when he says that he is. Others may say that it is right that one should suffer pain; but that he is suffering it is clear, that it is bad in itself is not to be denied. And the same goes for the positive side, pleasure. Given these clear and indubitable definitions of Good and Bad, Bentham went out into the world to correct prison abuses, to reform political institutions, and to codify the laws so as to exhibit patterns of justice. Right was reduced to the status of means, to be judged by a "felicific calculus." There was a Right but it was not autonomous. This instrumentalism does deference, but only in its own way, to the concept of Rightness. Right as autonomous was believed to be iniquitous. Goodness is safer, and Rightness thus disciplined gets correction in the teleology of the Good.

Bentham made a slashing attack, first upon Blackstone, who had elevated Right to the skies and had enthroned iniquity by equating Right with Reasonable and Reasonable with the law as it then and there prevailed. "So great," opined Blackstone, "is the regard of the law for private property, that it will not authorize the least violation of it, not even for the general good of the whole community." Later Bentham broadened his attack along the whole front of theory, elevating what he conceived the "general good of the whole community" to be the corrective test of every claim of Right. So Bentham flays every form of intuitionism and all the symbols to which the intuitive affixes itself: "asceticism," "sympathy," "antipathy," "law of nature," "will of God," "Right Reason," and a host of other "fictions" as he called them—figments of imagination which, he thought, stood between men and the fulfilment of their desires for pleasure.

Of course men should do right, but Right is to be figured rationally in terms of causal knowledge which maximizes the Good. Here begins a most interesting story which we must tell, even at the pains of great abbreviation. The first step in the story is Bentham's discovery that just happiness (conceived as pleasure) was not enough. What is required as a moral standard is "the greatest happiness." The second step is his discovery that it must indeed be "the greatest happiness of the greatest number." This second step was in advance of the stage which Hutcheson had reached in calling for "the greatest happiness *for* the greatest number." The "for" suggests an authoritative order in which happiness is the commodity to be distributed from on high. That this was indeed the implication of Bentham's predecessor is made clear enough by Hutcheson's further description. In declaring that "virtue is in proportion to the number of persons to whom the happiness shall extend," Hutcheson specifically adds in parenthesis the fateful exception: "and here," he says, "the dignity or moral importance of persons may compensate numbers." It little matters, so long as this exception stands, that he makes "virtue . . . a compound ratio of the quantity of good and the number of enjoyers." *One* can outweigh a multitude, and so "greatest happiness" might be independent of "the greatest number."

Now the discernment by Bentham that social invidiousness was as perverse as wrong standards themselves, represented a great advance in his theory. It surprised him to have to make this discovery. He admits that he thought the upper class in power had only to have their attention called to wrongs existing to be willing and eager to correct them. This surprised him after the half century mark of his life: that men had to be pressured into reform of such obvious evils as prison sadism and electoral dishonesty. But having discovered how invidiousness operates—whether of "dignity" or of "moral importance"—Bentham celebrates its cure in the formulation that would prevent any favored few from getting a disproportionate share of good, on any claim of their differential superiority. The majority principle must prevail, and the majority must be counted in: it is to be "the greatest happiness *of the greatest number*." This gets the majority in, but it also, alas, may leave the minority out. How can any man be left out, since every man is a center of pleasure, which alone is good, and of pain, which alone is bad?

Here Bentham runs squarely afoul of the difficulty of who is to judge, a difficulty so grave that he was driven all the way to, through, and beyond the majority, all the way to, through, and beyond aristocracy; he was driven to radical individualism. Each man is his own judge, since each man knows better than others his own pleasures and pains. But is this not "pure democracy," i.e., a pure impossibility? Representative government is the best we can manage in a crowded world. Very well, then, the machinery of representation must be renovated (the Reform Bill of 1832), the administration of law must be impartial (prison and other administrative reforms), and the theory of representation must be so clarified and purified as to reduce to the minimum the evils of unbalanced pressures. Most of all and first of all, since sometimes some must judge for others, the basis of that judgment must radically exclude all social invidiousness. Having come all the way, Bentham now loads his formula with its last and weightiest phrase: "each to count for one and nobody for more than one."

There theory goes as far as theory can to make Right the faithful servant of the Good. But let us spell this fact out completely, for here we approach center. Starting with a radical preference for the Good and a radical determination to subordinate the Right, Bentham has been driven by defects in his Economy of the Good, so to say, to make Right equal to if not superior to the concept of the Good. The goodness of pleasure is seen to depend upon its proper implementation, and that implementation implies right accounting: it is not mere happiness, but it must be "the greatest happiness." Nor is that by itself enough: it must be of "the greatest number." Nor is that sufficient: it is all that as determined by a radical obligation: namely, that "each shall count for one and nobody for more than one." Now that is a different story. Not only does this procedure raise Right to a sort of guardianship over the Good; it gives Right the same sort of constitution as that given it by Bentham's theoretical enemy, Immanuel Kant. Indeed the two notions are now almost one and the same. They both raise individualism to the skies, and both would implement the doctrine by the application to practice of a radical equalitarianism as between individuals. Kant's Categorical Imperative—*"Act so as to use humanity, whether in your own person or in the person of another, always as an end, never as merely a means"*—is now without any obviously significant change become Bentham's demand. What else does Kant's maxim mean than that "each shall count for one and nobody for more than one"?

Let us not say that Bentham's teleology has become jural, nor that his Good is now become a Right. If we do not make it a question of "losing face," we will not have to make it a question of "saving face." But, truth to tell, Bentham has been driven by defense of his own position into a prescription for conduct, and a prescription which is to all intents and purposes the same as Kant's famous prescription. A quest for the full meaning of the Good, in all its dimensions, has landed Bentham far afield. It would not be too great a step, though Bentham does not take it, for him to claim in the end intuitive justification for his radical notion that nobody shall be counted out and, of those in, everybody shall count equally. How indeed could Bentham *prove* that this is the way it ought to be done? Is the prescription to pass, then, as a mere private prejudice, or as a large public prejudice, or is it self-evident, upon inspection, that equal treatment of all men is the minimal requirement of rationality?

It is not our present purpose to prove Sidgwick's claim that Bentham is as much in need of some *intuition* of equality as Kant was. Our purpose is merely to disclose at this stage the deep undertow of teleological ethics toward the Right, and to remark, in the case of Utilitarianism, how similar to Kantianism is the outcome. Without of necessity calling it "intuitionism" it is appropriate here to recall that John Stuart Mill worked this out to the same end as Sidgwick but more in keeping with the prejudices of his father, James Mill, and of Jeremy Bentham, mentor of both the

Mills. Taking their own associational psychology, Mill shows how, normally and naturally, conduct which initially has no hedonic quality (i.e. is not in itself good) *becomes* good by being frequently and rightly enough *associated* with what is pleasurable. But the most significant thing is that he does not stage his demonstration at the value-neutral level of Pavlov's dog, in which saliva as the pleasure-quotient is caused through "conditioning" to attach to and to flow from what earlier was as dry as the breasts of an octogenarian dowager. No, Mill proceeds, at a much higher level, to demonstrate how Duty, a mere means, can itself *become* an end, attractive in its own right. "Duty, stern daughter of the voice of God," this same duty can acquire such value potential as to justify martyrdom on (acquired) hedonic ground. It is because Mill saw how the Good can turn into the Right, how indeed Right can become one's highest good, because of this for a fact that he could believe it better to be a saint at the stake than a swine at the trough, "better to be Socrates dissatisfied," as he says, "than a pig satisfied." This is Kantianism arrived at, so to say, *a posteriori*. It is a riding of the argument to "where extremes meet," in the laudable effort to be fair. How close Mill comes to "intuitionism" one may judge for himself in the light of Mill's own summary: "When, therefore, those feelings and judgments declare the pleasure derived from the higher faculties to be preferable *in kind* apart from the question of intensity, to those of which the animal nature, disjoined from the higher faculties is susceptible, they are entitled on this subject to the same regard."

We need only to remind ourselves, in closing this section, that G. E. Moore who sharply sets Right apart from the Good finds it both so necessary and so impossible to achieve the Right that he identifies it with Custom and then proceeds practically to renounce the potency of Good to enable one to deal critically with Custom at all. He reaches by astute indirection what Bentham with courage and Mill with magnanimity sought to create: a functional union of the Right and the Good.

AFFINITY OF THE RIGHT FOR THE GOOD

Nor is the outcome substantially different if we start from the other extreme. Immanuel Kant does, as we have seen, represent the opposite, in his emphasis upon the Right as the correct vantage for ethics. Not only must Right supersede the Good, but if there be any conscious motive to achieve the Good at all, then the Right is corrupted at its source, and so loses its moral identity. To be Right, obligation must be done for no other motive than that of duty. This aspect of Kant we have properly emphasized already.

But we have not put into proper focus as yet Kant's efforts to justify this moral austerity. Let us put into reverse now the strategy of our discussion of Kant in Chapter 5. In the earlier effort we were trying to build to what Kant reaches by starting with what the student has to begin with. We worked up from the Good will to what is better than any Good, namely the Right. This final and austere Rightness proved to be not altogether adequate to the demands. The student is farther advanced now. So let us work downward, therefore, to celebrate Kant's two-way world. Kant, it will be recalled, recognized the motive of the Good by distinguishing between "supreme good," which is the acceptance of the Right, and "complete good," which would be the reward of the Right with the unearned increment of happiness. That is, Kant sees that it would not be a satisfactory world in which men were merely rational; it would be a better world where men did their duty not for happiness' sake but from the doing of which they nevertheless reaped happiness. This is surely to recognize Bentham's point and is to honor it in life considered as a two-way whole rather than merely as a temporal venture: as if one could compromise eternity without corrupting time!

Theologically speaking, Kant appears little different from Bentham. Kant's total ethical purview is a sort of *divine* hedonism. Happiness is a good, and it is a good that is goal of the Right, provided only God arrange it so. And God will arrange it so. Extremes meet, but this time meet in heaven. There are indications, however, even on earth, as to how far Kant was driven toward the notion that Good is indispensable to an ethics. The most obvious indication was earlier touched upon, Kant's use of the category "good" in connection with the will: nothing unequivocally good except a good will. But such a will *is* good, and it is unequivocally good, according to Kant. We saw, however, how Kant turned this beginning to the ending labelled Rightness only. He did it by disclosing that what makes the good will good is that it wills the Right. The content is all consistency; the form remains anomalous. Noting this, we passed by as irrelevant to our purpose then any emphasis upon the inconsistency.

It is relevant that we here observe more carefully the bearing of Kant's preoccupation with the will. Kant could have found his law, and could have kept it intact, by crediting final obligation to the will of God, as was highly respectable. Why did Kant not detach his doctrine from human relativism altogether and derive it from this source superior to man's will? He had too much regard for the dignity of man to make man less than autonomous. But to be morally autonomous, man must create the law which he obeys. The law has to do, moreover, with others as well as with himself. The first form of it plays up its nature merely as law: *"Act in conformity with that maxim, and that maxim only, which you can at the same time will to be a universal law."* That sounds like a law as law, regardless of its fruits, so only it be law-at-large. But note now the progress toward Bentham as Kant gives successive formulation to his fuller intent. The second draft of his Categorical Imperative reads: *"Act as if the maxim from which you act were to become through your will a universal law of nature."* You are now not merely a lawgiver for yourself, you see, but one with responsibility for a domain, the whole of nature. The third form spells this out much more concretely, now including humanity in its ambit: *"Act so as to use humanity, whether in your own person or in the person of another, always as an end, never as merely a means."* Here we have a human community as fruitage of the law as such, and a community which is, as the world has said and as Kant intended, democratic in its mutuality. Here is a law so much more than mere form that it envisages as content what Kant himself later in his treatise describes as "a kingdom of ends."

The Good Will which begins by having its nature merely in affirming law as such, ends by prescribing not merely a self-sustaining state of nature but also a self-sufficing society of man. Kant who meets Bentham in Heaven in the shadow of "the complete good," journeys far toward meeting every form of teleological ethics by a categorical imperative which evolves from law as law (compatible with autocracy) to law-as-end, compatible only with democracy: "each to count for one and nobody for more than one," as Bentham would approvingly say of Kant's world.

We may now generalize our two-fold illustration of the meeting of extremes in ethical theory: *every doctrine of the Right tends, out of deference to the Good, and every doctrine of the Good tends, out of defference to the Right, to lose each its sharp identity, in an ambivalence between clarity and completeness.*

I would present you as closing this discussion of the ebb-and-flow of ethical concepts, a novel notion of the value fundamental. Dynamically aware of both our historic motives—the Right and the Good—this hypothesis normalizes as natural and inherent a commonalty which they discover arduously and unintentionally, and which they reveal only through the struggles in which extremes meet, as it were, against their wills.

THE GOLDEN MEAN OF "BETTERMENT"

Suppose that neither of these notions—neither Right nor Good, I mean —were basic to ethics, what then? Well, it would be surprising, to say the least—surprising because so long overlooked. One or the other of these concepts has, with hardly an exception, been regarded as the value final. If both be disallowed, would ethics then not have to give up its pretension to being an independent "science" or discipline—would it not, that is, have to seek its definitions in terms of theology or biology or psychology? That would be the easy assumption but a premature one, as we shall now suggest. There is indeed another alternative, and it has been disclosed and developed, though perhaps not yet to completion, by an American scholar, Professor A. P. Brogan, of the University of Texas. It is a *relational* theory of ethics. (*Journal of Philosophy* XVI (1919):96.)

Unlike both Plato and G. E. Moore, from whom together this theory originally derived, Brogan holds that the basic value concept is neither a quality nor an entity. Like Moore's quality, Brogan's relation is indefinable, and for the same reason; but Good is not its name. Unlike Plato, to whom the theory is also indebted, Brogan holds that the basic value term is not an entity, such as the Form of the Good. Unlike Kant, Brogan holds that the basic moral notion is not an obligation of any sort. None of these, the final value term is a relation: the comparative "better—than," or "betterness," for short. This concept is ethically *autonomous* (not definable, that is, in other than moral terms); it is *basic* (not definable, that is, in other moral terms); it is *primitive* (not definable at all, that is, because too simple to permit of analysis); and indeed it is *unique* (being what it is, indeed, and not another thing).

If all this could be made out, it would be interesting and might prove important. We prefer, confined as we are to the scope of illustration, we prefer to indicate how fecund the notion is by merely showing to what account, definitional and otherwise, the relational theory can be put. The proof of this, as of any pudding, is the eating thereof.

If "betterness" is the fundamental term in ethics, then there is no other ethical term that can define it, and it in turn can be used to define all other ethical terms. Do you think of a term that can define "betterness"? If there is nothing outside of ethics which can define "betterness" (in psychology, like pleasure; or in biology, like adaptation; or in metaphysics, like reality or the whole; or in theology, like holiness or the will of God), then not only have we touched bottom with "betterness," but ethics stands forth not a discipline derived from some other science but as in that sense at least a somewhat in its own right, resting securely on its own autonomous foundation.

There is another "if" of importance to the student. It is this: if ethics is an autonomous enterprise and if its conceptual basis is this indicated relation of "betterness," then all other ethical terms should be definable through the use of this fundamental conception. It can be done, and Brogan proceeds to do it. Thus: *Good* is what had better be than not. *Bad* is what had better not be than be. *Right* is that than which nothing had better be done. *Wrong* is that which had better not be done than done. And *Duty* is that which had better be done than all else. (The distinction between "Right" and "Duty" is slight but theoretically important; it is the difference of alternative goods as compared with exclusive goods.)

Apart from the neat dialectics of it, this theory calls attention to a matter which is synoptic in its reach. Ethics is relative in a more fundamental sense than the anthropologists have taught us to believe. It is relative in its historic setting; it is relational, too, in its very logical structure. There is no room in ethics, therefore, for simple dogmatism. Moral things are not, as Bishop Butler thought, "what they are and will be what they will be." Rather, they are in relation between plural values, having their structure in their function and drawing their function not from contemplation but from comparison. Things are not really what they are as simple characters, but they are what they are as relations between value factors. "There could be no value at all," says Brogan, "unless there were several valuables, one of which is better than another." "Better and worse," says he again, "are simply different ways of talking about the same relation." Professor Brogan has taught us, upon this basis, that there need not be a "highest" good or a "lowest" evil. There is only "betterness" and "worseness." Moral dogmatism suffers a solar plexus, and social invidiousness suffers an attack from the flanks.

In tune indeed with our democratic practice in America is this theoretical formulation. Without a privileged upper class than "whom there could be no whomer" and without a despised lower class than "which nothing could be whicher," America has been from the beginning, and remains, a sort of ubiquitous middle class. Public opinion polls have indicated from time to time that Americans think they belong to the "middle class," regardless of their differentia. Their thinking it so *makes* it so. There's no social distinction of low or high but invidiousness makes it so. Before fish, said Herbert Hoover, "all men are equal." Naked, no men are superior—nor women either. If "a man's a man for a' that and a' that," he is to be judged, and he judges himself, against his own record or by the records of his peers, not in terms of some "loaded" standard mediated by others and manipulated to the end of their own deference.

All this Professor Brogan's theory seems to betoken. Others have played at the fringes of relativism, he thrusts to the focus of relationality. His is a constitutional stroke. Betterness (or worseness) it is which invests with whatever meaning they have all attributions of good and bad, all presumptions of right and wrong. This rendition leaves men to be judged against one another, and puts each man in wholesome competition with himself. It is this which is required to give a firm logical core to Dewey's remark that "the good man is the man who no matter how morally unworthy he has been is moving to become better." No resting on laurels in the life of aspiration, nor any surrender before previous failures. Such a view inestimably lowers the floor on fanaticism and incalculably raises the ceiling on dogmatism. There is no top or bottom to the moral scale; there is only the indefinitely expansible middle.

Here is an ethics which is truly "constructive." Where all is relational in extent, all becomes comparative in intent. Such a point of view not only furthers the type of meeting of extremes, which we have just illustrated, but, by regularizing the approach, makes progressive and fruitful the impulse toward completeness. It yields us a *constructive* ethics indeed. In a nut-shell such an ethics means: "When you stop being better, you stop being good."

THE WAY TO GET IS TO FORGET

Our ethical pilgrimage is over. Let us glance at the way we have come together, seeing now only the successive summits and them in the easy perspective of hindsight. So regarded, what appears as the "moral" of our study of Morality? Twofold. It is, in general, this: that nothing which we have learned is ever wholly lost; *but, in particular, this also:* that we shall be wiser when we have assimilated our knowledge and better when we have forgotten it.

Nothing so becomes virtue as spontaneity, to which knowledge is but introduction and assimilation the enlarged pursuit. What better becomes the good man than that he be unconscious of his goodness?—and what can so raise Rightness to magnanimity—that king of virtues—as that duty be done noiselessly? The moralist who thinks that he is as good as he ought to be, is not as good as he ought to be.

What we have learned is variegated, and the present elements of our future wisdom may jossle one another in the limbo of our minds, to which shadowland and complex will quickly enough, and wholesomely enough, be now consigned. From the jostling incident to our further journeying, moreover, there will sink down the substantial sediment of each theory; and those residues together—for they will make their own harmony as they mix, do we not spy too suspiciously on the process— will build bone for the marrow of our sensitivity and will provide arteries for the blood of our desires. Eclecticism achieves true synthesis only in each integrated individual's philosophy of life. What the moral synthesis is to be may now well be left, as of course it must be left, to you—to you and Fate. Fate, when approached in this sporting spirit, slinks away and leaves you with yourself—and free.

It is possible—and this is our last suggestion, offered hesitatingly enough

since it is now your business—that instead of mingling to form one m
single and the same for all, as moralists have ever hoped, the final outco
of such assimilation may be a strategy of succession befitting the seve
Ages of Man, until each Age selects as its own catalyst the theory most
commensurate with its powers. To illustrate this pluralistic surmise, the
puling infant will honor Hedonism as his own, sucking pleasure from hi
"erogenous zones," as eager lips play host to active thumb. The matur
youth will reluctantly but appreciatively accept the Right, to give bou
aries to his now habitual Good, and may be left confidently (if w
mannered) to pick and choose and combine as he can the several in
gredients of duty. The middle-aged will find in the Golden Mean of duty
not underdone and of good not overdone the meaning of morality. The
aged will see combined all elements, all watered down, accepted w th
natural piety, and put to the uses of magnanimity: desires at last sa
accepted as guides because disciplined by life into tolerable duties.

Be this the outcome, or otherwise, let the process of living go ah
ever ahead, and go ahead without fear. It is the nature of life to overflo
its categories, even its moral categories. "You are not alone," as the wise
American Commandant used to say to the "democratized" German Pris-
oners of War as they departed for their hard homeland. Veritably, no
man is alone. All the beasts of prey, alas, abide within him for noctu *l*
company and prowl for sport through man's arteries when desires *e*
high. All that men have learned is, luckily, before each man in cust ns
and within him as habits. Vaguer promptings peer through the windows
of his growing conscience. Laws furnish bannisters to the bridges that
reason must negotiate between the chasms of untamed appetites. And
high surmise giving tone to all desire, substantializing every aspirati n,
pushes ever for metamorphosis into the successive haloes that "the divi e"
provides as lures for pilgrim feet. Intimations these, and all, of somethin
categorical in essence, creative in content, informing with appreciatio
all that has been, as man reaches forward to all that may yet be.

SPECTRUM  PAPERBACKS

*Other SPECTRUM Books . . . quality paperbacks that
meet the highest standards of scholarship and integrity.*

S-1   THE CAUSES OF THE CIVIL WAR, Kenneth M. Stampp, $1.75

S-2   IMMIGRATION AS A FACTOR IN AMERICAN HISTORY, Oscar Handlin, $1.95

3   PSYCHOANALYSIS AND PSYCHOTHERAPY—36 SYSTEMS, Robert A. Harper, $1.95

S-4   FALLACY—THE COUNTERFEIT OF ARGUMENT, W. Ward Fearnside and William B. Holther, $1.95

5   THE GREAT DEBATE—OUR SCHOOLS IN CRISIS, C. Winfield Scott, Clyde M. Hill, and Hobert W. Burns, $1.95

6   FREEDOM AND CULTURE, Dorothy Lee, $1.95

S-7   UNDERSTANDING TODAY'S THEATRE, Edward A. Wright, $1.95

S-8   GOLDEN AGES OF THE THEATER, Kenneth Macgowan and William Melnitz, $1.95

S-9   THE SEARCH FOR AMERICA, edited by Huston Smith, *paper* $1.95, *cloth* $2.95

S-10   THE GREAT DEPRESSION, edited by David A. Shannon, $1.95

S-11   WHAT PRICE ECONOMIC GROWTH? edited by Klaus Knorr and William J. Baumol, *paper* $1.95, *cloth* $3.95

S-12   SCARCITY AND EVIL, Vivian Charles Walsh, *paper* $1.95, *cloth* $3.95

S-13   JUSTICE AND SOCIAL POLICY, Frederick Olafson, $1.95

14   CONSTRUCTIVE ETHICS, T. V. Smith and William Debbins, $1.95

15   LONELINESS, Clark E. Moustakas, *paper* $1.95, *cloth* $3.75

16   KNOWLEDGE: ITS VALUES AND LIMITS, Gustave Weigel, S.J., and Arthur G. Madden, *paper* $1.75, *cloth* $3.75

17   THE EDUCATION OF TEACHERS, G. K. Hodenfield and T. M. Stinnett, *paper* $1.95, *cloth* $3.95

S-18   LITERATURE, POPULAR CULTURE, AND SOCIETY, Leo Lowenthal, $1.95

19   PARADOX AND PROMISE: ESSAYS ON AMERICAN LIFE AND EDUCATION, Harry S. Broudy, *paper* $1.95, *cloth* $3.95

20   RELIGION IN AMERICA: PAST AND PRESENT, Clifton E. Olmstead, $1.95

21   RELIGION AND THE KNOWLEDGE OF GOD, Gustave Weigel, S.J., and Arthur G. Madden, *paper* $1.95, *cloth* $3.95

The American Assembly Series

S-AA-1 THE FEDERAL GOVERNMENT AND HIGHER EDUCATION, edited by Douglas M. Knight, *paper* $1.95, *cloth* $3.50
S-AA-2 THE SECRETARY OF STATE, edited by Don K. Price, *paper* $1.95, *cloth* $3.50
S-AA-3 GOALS FOR AMERICANS, THE REPORT OF THE PRESIDENT'S COMMISSION ON NATIONAL GOALS, *paper,* $1.00, *cloth* $3.50
S-AA-4 ARMS CONTROL: ISSUES FOR THE PUBLIC, edited by Louis Henkin, *paper* $1.95, *cloth* $3.50

Science and Technology Series

S-ST-1 THE ATOM AND ITS NUCLEUS, George Gamow, *paper* $1.95, *cloth* $3.75
S-ST-2 ROCKET DEVELOPMENT, Robert H. Goddard, *paper* $2.45, *cloth* $3.95

Classics in History Series

S-CH-1 FRONTIER AND SECTION: SELECTED ESSAYS OF FREDERICK JACKSON TURNER, Introduction and notes by Ray Allen Billington, *paper* $1.95, *cloth* $3.95
S-CH-2 DRIFT AND MASTERY: AN ATTEMPT TO DIAGNOSE THE CURRENT UNREST, Walter Lippman, Introduction and notes by William E. Leuchtenburg, $1.95
S-CH-3 THE NEW NATIONALISM, Theodore Roosevelt, Introduction and notes by William E. Leuchtenburg, $1.95
S-CH-4 THE NEW FREEDOM: A CALL FOR THE EMANCIPATION OF THE GENEROUS ENERGIES OF A PEOPLE, Woodrow Wilson, Introduction and notes by William E. Leuchtenburg, $1.95
S-CH-5 SELECTED CORRESPONDENCE OF JOHN ADAMS AND THOMAS JEFFERSON, Introduction and notes by Zoltán Haraszti, *paper* $2.25, *cloth* $3.95
S-CH-6 THE SUPREME COURT AND THE CONSTITUTION, Charles A. Beard, Introduction by Alan Westin, *paper* $1.95, *cloth* $3.95